Life Mastery

Beyond My Calling

Wanda Marie

Beyond My Calling

Copyright © 2025 by Wanda Marie

Creating New Realities Publications

All rights reserved. Printed in the United States of America. Except as permitted under the United States Copyright Act, no part of this manual may be reproduced or distributed in any form or by any means, including internet or podcast, or stored in a database or retrieval system, without prior written permission of the author.

For information about permission to reproduce selections from this manual and any supplemental or supporting documents, write to:

Legacy Lifestyles LLC
2153 Brevard Rd
Arden, NC 28704
CoachWandaMarie@gmail.com
www.CoachWandaMarie.com

ISBN: 978-0-9797215-9-5

> **Warning:** This book is NOT AI-generated. It is SI-generated (Spiritually Inspired) and may contain truth and irregular speech patterns.

A Special Thank You!

To my wonderful husband, Ron Lapointe, and dear friend, Jennifer Lanning, for taking the time to read my work, offering valuable insights, and loving feedback.

And to the first group of ladies who allowed me to guide them on the six-month Life Mastery journey, taking a deep dive into this work:

Leeann Carey
Melissa Webb
Tara Thomas
Tasha Rae Hunter

Dedicated to You!

It does not matter how broken you may feel, or how wealthy, successful, or popular you may be; if you are not at peace and not happy, you need the tools that *"Life Mastery"* has to offer. It's time to stop living a lie and own your truth, discover your true purpose, and embrace your calling. If you're ready to say "YES" to peace and happiness, this book is dedicated to YOU!

Table of Contents

INTRODUCTION 7

PART 1: THE FIVE STEPS TO JOY 13

    Step 1 – PURPOSE 16

    Step 2 – MINDSET 41

    Step 3 – EMOTIONS 47

    Step 4 – ACTIONS 51

    Step 5 – FULFILLMENT 55

PART II: THE LIFE MASTERY SYSTEM™ 57

    WHAT IS LIFE MASTERY 58

    DAILY PRACTICE SHEET 60

    WEEKLY TRACKING 63

    SUSTAINABILITY 65

PART III: THE JOURNEY OF AWAKENING 71

    HOW LIFE WORKS 73

    LEVEL 1 - THE DREAMER (Waking Up) 81

    LEVEL 2 - THE CREATOR (Eyes Opened) 107

    LEVEL 3 - THE SEEKER (Aware) 117

    LEVEL 4 - THE SERVANT (Fully Awake) 125

PART IV – BEYOND THE CALLING 139

    BEYOND MY CALLING 141

    VOICE OF THE MASTER 146

    ABOUT THE AUTHOR 167

Beyond My Calling

INTRODUCTION

As a woman who has a rich and rewarding life but grew up in poverty, surviving domestic violence, incest, and depression, I'm on a mission to inspire and educate women that, regardless of your past experiences or current circumstances, you too can create an amazing life for yourself going forward. This book contains all the tools I used to transform my dysfunctional world into one of beauty.

My work is typically focused on helping women heal as we are rather emotional beings, and studies show that twice as many women as men experience depression. Ladies, we've got to do better. We've got to find our purpose, our reason for being, then follow our hearts and begin to experience and express the fullness of joy through us, as us, based on our Soul's desires. We've got to come alive!

Women are wired to please, so women often get caught up in living someone else's dream, be it their parents', their partner's, or whatever society claims for them. Strong-minded young women often rebel against what others want for them and forge their own paths. However, many women will remain complacent for years before standing up and deciding for themselves what they genuinely want from life and asking the critical question, "What does life want from me?"

Women are often wired to serve, so once they enter a committed relationship, they usually lose themselves in service to their partner. If the relationship ends, they experience resentment because they have given their all to it, believing their happiness lies within it. It does not. Happiness lies within you. You can only know true happiness when you know why you are here, the reason you were born, and you have a mission to fulfill your purpose in life. When you know who you are and you are in a relationship with someone who knows who they are, you can support and empower each other. Then, you have truly found your life partner, and life becomes beautiful. It's easier for women to find their purpose and commit to their passions before finding their life partner.

Your purpose may be to make some significant discoveries that will change the course of humanity, or simply raise a family. Your purpose may be to heal the sick, care for children, animals, trees, gardens, prepare delicious meals that nurture, work in the legal system, build buildings, or plant trees. You may have been born to draw or paint pictures, capture art in photographs, sing songs, educate others, or build businesses. Only you can know what's truly in your heart, what lights you up and drives you to want to jump out of bed early each day.

Men are also wired to please and to serve, but not from the same place as women. Men are driven more by ego, and their need to please or serve tends to stem from ego satisfaction. Women's desire to please and/or serve typically stems from the heart, motivated by love, the need for acceptance, or a desire for connection.

I Said "YES" to a Beautiful My Life!

I have a beautiful life. I'm constantly being told that my life seems magical. And I feel like I have it all. I have an amazing husband, great relationships with my kids, a lovely home in the Blue Ridge Mountains of Asheville, NC, plus a vacation home in Florida where we spend our winters. I'm the author of several self-help books, and I've been helping women transform their lives for more than 25 years. At a young age, I learned to reclaim my power and take ownership of my life. I started with nothing and have truly created a beautiful life for myself.

I grew up in South Central Los Angeles. My parents were barely able to keep a roof over our heads. Mom was a raging alcoholic, always armed with a knife and a gun, both of which she used. My stepdad felt it was his duty to try to tame her by challenging her to fist fights that often led to bloodshed. He also thought it was his duty to start teaching me about sex from age 5 until I turned 10 and found the courage to speak up. My mother refused to believe what was happening and suggested I didn't speak of this to anyone. I was shut down, my voice unheard, my heart ached.

At 17, I left home pregnant by the boy next door, got a job at Job Corps, and vowed never to return home again. My baby's father begged me for months before I finally said yes and married him. I was too messed up mentally and emotionally to say yes when he first asked. I didn't trust him; I didn't trust men. I didn't trust myself; I didn't trust anyone.

I was so depressed, I eventually sought therapy – that didn't help. It didn't answer the questions I had. What's it all about? Why was I in so much pain? I started seeking truth. What is love? What is God? What is real? Who am I, and why am I here? I read the Bible cover to cover twice! I studied various world religions and different spiritual practices. Back in the day, there was a metaphysical bookstore on Melrose Avenue in Los Angeles called the Bodhi Tree. I lived at the Bodhi Tree, where I could hang out, sip tea, read, and study different theologies, as well as attend seminars and workshops on spirituality.

I read every spiritual and metaphysical book I could get my hands on. I went to every free workshop I could find and listened to audio lectures from spiritual "New Thought" leaders. I learned that **we create our own realities. Wait – What! You mean I created the horrible environment I was brought up in? What! You mean we choose our parents?** It all began to make sense once I was willing to take full responsibility for my life's experiences, which sounds totally crazy! However, I continued to study everything. Over the years, I mastered how to apply the Universal Laws and Spiritual Principles that govern our lives to reclaim my power from the pain of my past. This once trauma-stricken little girl from a totally dysfunctional household became a very empowered young lady who has created a beautiful and magical life for herself.

Of course, I learned how to create material things, such as wonderful homes, cars, vacations, and travel. However, more importantly, I created loving relationships, a deep spiritual connection, and I found my purpose and embraced my calling, empowering other women to create beautiful lives.

Not just women, but many people today suffer from health challenges due to the stress of being dissatisfied with their careers, businesses, finances, relationships, and overall sense of purpose and direction in life. For over 25 years, I have dedicated my life to inspiring and empowering people to reclaim their power and take control of their lives, ultimately achieving true fulfillment.

This book will guide you through the fundamental tools and powerful advanced practices for achieving deep personal growth, transformation, and life mastery. You must explore these teachings with an open mind, willing to challenge your beliefs, and ready to manifest the magic you desire in your life.

Regardless of whether you are male or female, or where you are on your path, this book will provide you with valuable tools and insights to manage your mind and emotions, helping you begin to master your life by defining who you truly are, what you truly want, and the gifts and talents you are here to share with the world.

Welcome

Dear Sisters and Brothers on the Path,

I'm in awe of you, and I'm honored that you are allowing me to be your guide on this very sacred journey. View this journey as a rite of passage, for it is long overdue.

To be successful on this journey, you must be willing to see things from a different perspective. **Everything is perception.** How you see your past will determine your future. Be willing to change your perception of the past so that you might create a future worthy of your greater potential, your amazing love, and heartfelt generosity.

As my friend Les Brown says, "You were born for greatness!" DREAM BIG!!! Don't be afraid, for **it is within your dreams that your Soul speaks to you!** It is within your willingness to dream big that your greater potential as a spiritual being becomes realized here on earth.

To aid you in dreaming big, from the book "A Happy Pocket Full of Money" by David Cameron Gikandi, I invite you to begin this journey by writing down 100 goals you would like to see unfold in your lifetime. Do not put chains on your imagination. Let your mind soar! It's easy to come up with 100 wishes when you include the details. If you want to learn to play the piano, decide what type of piano, who you would like to study with, where you see yourself playing, etc.? You were meant for so much more than you had previously imagined. Read your list every day during your Life Mastery journey. That one single act will transform your life beyond your beliefs. Trust the process.

Our journey's guiding pledge is to **bless the past, embrace the present,** and **trust the future.**

I BLESS the PAST as it has taught me valuable lessons and shown me my strength and courage, and the power to rise above anything.

I EMBRACE the PRESENT as it is the only thing that's truly happening, and I am safe, aware, and surrendering to my greater yet to be.

I TRUST the FUTURE for it is in God's hands, and I vow to follow my guidance with grace and ease. Regardless of appearances or circumstances, I KNOW all is well.

The key to Life Mastery is learning to manage your mind and your emotions, so the distractions of this world do not rob you of who you truly are and all that you have come here to give.

It all begins with finding what brings you joy, then embracing your Soul's calling.

I love you,

Wanda Marie

PART 1: THE FIVE STEPS TO JOY

These are the first five steps to a life-long journey of peace and happiness!

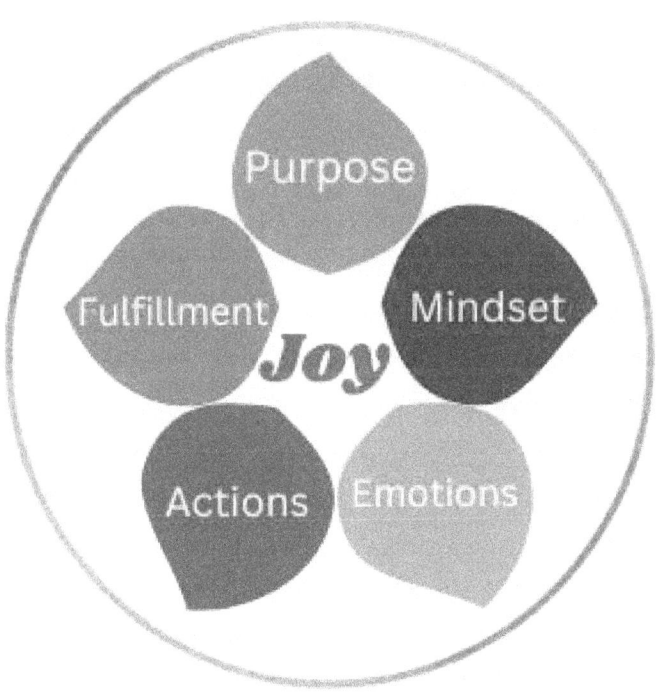

Beyond My Calling

Life Mastery

Life Mastery is about finding and sustaining peace and happiness to **allow the fullness of JOY** to be expressed through you, as you, based on your Soul's desires.

Joy stems from a sense of accomplishment, feeling useful and productive, which boosts confidence, self-esteem, and a desire to be, do, and share more. This allows for experiencing a more meaningful and joyful life.

Without joy, the Soul becomes depressed, and if long-term depression sets in, the Soul wants to exit the body, as there is no sense of purpose, no joy, and no reason for living.

The foundation of the Life Mastery System™ is based on "The Five Steps to Joy."

The Five Steps to Joy

1. **Purpose:** You need a **REASON** for being, for living.
2. **Mindset:** Your thoughts must be in ALIGNMENT with your purpose.
3. **Emotions:** Your feelings must be in ALIGNMENT with your thoughts.
4. **Actions:** Your actions are determined by your thoughts and feelings.
5. **Fulfillment:** Your mission is to fulfill your purpose through your actions. **GIVE** what you came to give, and/or do what you came to do.

STEP 1 – PURPOSE

Know what lights you up, drives your dreams, and moves you into action.

Step One – Purpose is the biggest step you'll take. To allow the fullness of joy to be expressed through you, you must begin by knowing your purpose in life, what turns you on. Then learn to manage your mind and emotions to stay on the path that leads to true peace and happiness.

Start by asking yourself these questions:

1. What was my childhood dream of becoming when I grew up?
   _____
   _____

2. What are my natural talents (what do others say is my claim to fame)?
   _____
   _____

3. What activities bring me the most joy (not external happiness, but internal joy)?
   _____
   _____
   _____

4. What is one major problem in the world that really disturbs me to my core?
   _____
   _____
   _____

5. What could I do for the world that would bring me a deep sense of joy and satisfy my Soul?
   _____
   _____
   _____

6. If I had all the time, money, and resources to do what I want to do, what legacy would I leave?
   _____
   _____
   _____

7. What is the gift that I am here to share with the world (my true purpose)?
   _____
   _____
   _____

When you focus on the "activities" that bring you joy, you will find that you have a natural talent and become good at those activities. You'll notice those activities also align with your values.

As you participate more in the activities that bring joy to your soul, you may become passionate about them, developing a desire to share them with the world in some manner.

What brings you joy?
What lights you up and turns you on?

"I used to think purpose meant finding one grand mission or external achievement. Now I understand that my purpose is to live as fully, honestly, and compassionately as I can, and to turn my liberation into light for others. Each act of courage, kindness, or authenticity ripples outward in ways I may never see, but I trust that it matters."

Leeann Carey, Life Mastery Graduate

The Truth of Your Desires

Knowing your purpose and why you're here is the first step. Knowing what you TRULY want opens you up to discovering the deeper desires of your Soul.

Energy follows the path of least resistance. Being aligned with the truth of your desires dissipates any obstacles in your path.

What is the truth of your desires? Do you want the coat, or the warmth the coat provides? Do you want the money, or the things that money can buy? Do you want marriage or the comfort and convenience that marriage may offer? What is the truth of your desires?

Desires of the heart reveal clues to your calling. When you start to envision the possibilities, you begin to get clear about the experiences you'd like to have in life and how you want to show up.

Start by creating a vision statement for each item below, then set goals to achieve your vision.

1. The vision for my **CAREER / BUSINESS** is:
   _____
   _____

2. The vision for my **MONEY / FINANCIAL HEALTH** is:
   _____
   _____

3. The vision for my **HEALTH and FITNESS** is:
   _____
   _____

4. The vision for my **FAMILY and FRIENDS** is:
   _____
   _____

5. The vision for my **SIGNIFICANT OTHER / LOVE LIFE** is:
   _____
   _____

6. The vision for my **SPIRITUAL / PERSONAL GROWTH** is:
   _____
   _____

7. The vision for having more **FUN and RECREATION** is:
   _____
   _____

8. The vision for my **PHYSICAL ENVIRONMENT** *(home and car)* is:

_____
_____

Be flexible and realize that your visions
will evolve as you grow.

Now that you have identified visions for different areas of your life, it's time to set some goals for bringing your dreams into reality. This gives your mind something to focus on as you create a brighter future. Later, you will be asked to release your goals to surrender to something greater. But for now, this is an essential step in taking back your power and control of your life.

The mind is always working on your behalf, but it needs clear and positive direction. Because we know there is something more powerful, beyond our mind, with every goal we set, we always leave the door open by saying, "This or something better."

S.M.A.R.T. Goals

If you've never achieved big goals, it's easy to think, "This could never happen for me." However, it can —and it will — if you take small steps each day toward achieving your goals. We embrace our visions by setting S.M.A.R.T. goals.

A person who is not consciously aware might set lofty goals. As you awaken to a new reality, you'll want to set smart goals. **S.M.A.R.T. is an acronym for Specific, Measurable, Achievable, Relevant, and Time-based.**

Specific: What specifically do you want? Do you want a particular house to create a home, or are you looking for a place to stay that's just safe? Be clear and identify the truth of your desires by asking yourself, "What exactly do I want and why?"

Measurable. How will you know you've reached your goal? Let's say your goal is to get closer to your family. You might set a goal that's more action-oriented on your part that would draw you closer. Your goal might be to offer to host a game night once a week for a month. The act of "offering" is achieving your goal of getting closer. The number of times you offered is measurable.

Achievable: Do you have the knowledge, skills, and/or resources to achieve your goal? A S.M.A.R.T. goal is not dependent on anyone else. For example, your goal can't be to get a raise. That is not within your control. But your goal could be to ask for a raise.

Relevant. Look at the big picture and vision you're holding for your life. Does this goal make sense, or would it be a distraction? Stay focused and on purpose.

Time-based. When will you achieve this goal? Make sure to give yourself plenty of time. When we rush things, we often begin putting things off, and procrastination sets in. Be realistic in knowing when you can achieve your goal without struggling. When you reach a goal, be sure to check it off as DONE! This gives you motivation to keep going!

My goals for my **CAREER / BUSINESS** are:

_____ Due _____ Done _____

_____ Due _____ Done _____

_____ Due _____ Done _____

Life Mastery

My goals for my **MONEY / FINANCIAL HEALTH** are:

_____ Due _____ Done _____

_____ Due _____ Done _____

_____ Due _____ Done _____

My goals for my **HEALTH and FITNESS** are:

_____ Due _____ Done _____

_____ Due _____ Done _____

_____ Due _____ Done _____

My goals for my **FAMILY and FRIENDS** are:

_____ Due _____ Done _____

_____ Due _____ Done _____

_____ Due _____ Done _____

My goals for my **SIGNIFICANT OTHER / LOVE LIFE** are:

_____ Due _____ Done _____

_____ Due _____ Done _____

_____ Due _____ Done _____

My goals for my **SPIRITUAL / PERSONAL GROWTH** are:

_____ Due _____ Done _____

_____ Due _____ Done _____

_____ Due _____ Done _____

My goals for having more **FUN and RECREATION** are:

_____ Due _____ Done _____

_____ Due _____ Done _____

_____ Due _____ Done _____

My goals for my **PHYSICAL ENVIRONMENT** (home & car) are:

_____ Due _____ Done _____

_____ Due _____ Done _____

_____ Due _____ Done _____

S.M.A.R.T. Goal Verification: Verify each of your goals.

- **Specific:** What exactly will you accomplish?
- **Measurable:** How will you know you have reached this goal?
- **Achievable:** Do you have everything needed to achieve this goal?
- **Relevant:** Why is this goal significant to your life?
- **Timely:** When will you achieve this goal?

You have visions; you have goals. Now, dare to say "YES" to living out loud! Say "YES" to living your dreams! It takes courage to go beyond your so-called "norm." Be willing to step outside of your sandbox and play a bigger game. You are constantly creating your life's experiences —why not do so with conscious choice?

Conscious Creation

I talk to many people about living their dreams and following their hearts. There seem to be four basic types of attitudes: those who can't follow their dreams for whatever reason; those who are too lazy to do the work; those who want to but need guidance; and those who jump in and do it! What type of person are you?

My first conscious creation was when I was about 5 years old. I lay in bed with the lights on, afraid of the dark, and watched a giant Black Widow spider on the ceiling above my bed. I stared at it, and it stared back. I wanted to touch him and see how he felt. I wanted to play with him. I have total recall of drawing him to me. At one point, while staring at the ceiling, I realized the spider was gone. Within that exact moment, I became paralyzed. I tried screaming as pain rushed through my tiny body. No vocal sounds came forth. I could not move my body, and breathing became increasingly difficult. I passed out. I woke up in the hospital, wrapped in my favorite blanket. The only thought I can remember is 'WOW!' What an experience!

My second conscious creation was a blue bicycle. My mother and stepfather finally decided they could no longer live together without killing each other, so Mom and I were on our own. She landed a full-time live-in nursing job, and I ended up living with my grandparents. I asked for a red bicycle for Christmas. We could not afford it. But I had already seen the bike in my mind, and I wanted it. I saw myself riding this bicycle, even though I didn't know how to ride a bike at that time. I saw it very clearly and had so much fun using my imagination. Well, when my mother came to pick me up from my grandparents' home for Christmas, she had a man with her who wanted to impress her so much that he had bought a new bicycle for her daughter. YES! It was blue and not red as I had imagined – it was also a lot larger than I had imagined. But it was a brand-new bicycle, and I knew I had dreamed it into being.

By the time I got married at eighteen, I was already a master manifester. I knew how to dream up my world, even if I didn't have any money. I knew the power of visualization and manifestation. I tried to share the tools I used with my husband so he could stop struggling and become a better provider. Well, his idea of reality was quite different from mine; he believed that if anything was worth having, one had to work hard for it and be smarter than the next person.

I realized I couldn't rely on him for my happiness. So, I began using my tools, and over a period of 8 years, I created like crazy:

- I bought a car with no money down and no money in the bank.
- We moved from a low-income apartment in South Central Los Angeles to a luxury apartment in the Beach Cities, paying three times the rent. I had no job at the time we qualified.
- My husband managed to get laid off from work at the same time we decided to buy a house. That didn't stop me; my mind was made up to buy a house. In the bank, we had less than the cost of moving into another apartment. We looked at 3 houses, bought the third, and closed within 30 days.
- I created a brand-new Ford Mustang by visualizing it coming to me from the heavens by way of pink wings. That was fun.

- I created a brand-new tri-level home in Redondo Beach that I considered a mansion.
- I gave myself a $1000 salary increase by creating a new job title for myself.
- I cured myself of a yeast infection that had been my close friend every summer for years.

Before you can consciously create your life the way you want it, you must first know WHAT YOU WANT. I was always very clear about what I wanted, and I firmly believed I deserved it and would eventually receive it. I never worried or thought about how things would come about. I was raised as a poor person, without the traditional resources for attaining what I wanted. So, I had to rely on my creative imagination and faith.

Seven Elements of Conscious Creation

1. Getting really clear about what you want.
2. Believe that it will be good for all concerned.
3. Believe you SHOULD have it, you deserve to be happy.
4. Know with all your heart you will get it (faith).
5. Don't worry about HOW it will unfold (trust).
6. Maintain an attitude of gratitude for everything. EVERYTHING, the good, the bad, and the ugly.
7. Use the power of VAM (visualization, affirmations, and meditation) daily.

The Power of VAM *(Visualization, Affirmation, and Meditation*

When you have clear goals, there are two ways to manifest them: with ease or with effort. The way of the King requires physical energy and effort. The way of the Queen requires emotional energy with ease. Both ways work; the way of the Queen usually works the quickest, as there are no physical time constraints to deal with. Our society has been taught the way of the King: work hard and steadily, retire, and die.

The new age is bringing forth the awareness of the Goddess energies, where much is accomplished with grace and ease. These teachings are based on the way of grace and ease. It does not mean that there is no work involved; it simply means that physical struggle is not necessary. You only take action when guided by your intuition. Then you know your actions are timely, and you get the most out of the energy you put forth. You are working smart, not hard. This brings me to what I call the power of VAM.

After I knew what I wanted to create, I would use the power of VAM to get it. It wasn't until I was in my early 20s that I realized what I was actually doing. I would use my imagination (visualization), my natural tendency toward positive thinking (affirmations), and my intuition (through meditation). It was so easy and natural for me; it wasn't until after I was married that I really realized not everyone creates their life this way. What an awakening!

You may have tried visualization at some point in your life, affirmations that felt like lies, and meditations that felt unproductive. And perhaps you have used one or more of these tools with some degree of success. I am here to assure you that this works if you know how to use it.

To achieve what I wanted, I would visualize myself already having it —just the way I wanted it, with all the trimmings —each night as I drifted off to sleep. I could actually feel it; there was an emotional charge to being one with the image I was creating.

I created positive **AFFIRMATIONS** to reprogram my mind. If your mind thinks in a way that does not support your heart's desires because of logical reasoning, you lose. Whenever negative thoughts or doubts crept into my mind, I would repeat my positive affirmations to maintain a balanced state of mind. I would write it out 100 times if necessary, and/or make a song out of it, and sing it in my car. I walked all over doubt with positive thinking and the power of the spoken word.

I would **MEDITATE** for 10 to 15 minutes every morning. Simply sitting in silence and asking for guidance for the new day. Often, I would find someone in my life who would be instrumental in helping me attain my goals, or information would be provided without my asking, because most of the time, I never knew what to ask. I would find myself in the right place at the right time. Meditation always places you at the door, ready when opportunity knocks.

I want to share a gift I received from Dr. Wayne Dyer that helps train your mind to stay focused during meditation. First, remember that your mind has been in control of your life for a long time, and it is not going to relinquish that control easily. Surrender is a foreign word to the mind. Begin by visualizing the number 24 in your mind, represented in extremely large numbers. Then begin counting down from 24 to zero. Count down slowly. Whenever your mind gets off track, you start over again at 24. It may take a few days to reach zero, but once you do, you'll enter an alpha state of consciousness, becoming more open to meditation and inner guidance.

Visualization

Let's take a deep dive into VAM, beginning with visualization.

When people say they have a hard time visualizing, I ask what they had for breakfast or dinner, or what they wore to work yesterday. To access that information, they would need to "see" a picture in their mind. That is visualization. It's a normal function of the mind, and everyone does it.

Creative visualization is your strongest manifestation tool. The subconscious mind does not know the difference between fantasy and reality, so whatever you can impress upon the subconscious as true through imagination can ultimately come about for you.

Visualization involves creating a mental picture, which can be done at any time, preferably just before going to sleep. This allows you to take the vision with you into your deepest state of relaxation for greater impact on the subconscious mind.

Creative Visualization is the process of consciously creating an image in your mind that is not rooted in the past, but rather one that you are building for the future. Again, everyone does this, and so can you. It's also called daydreaming or fantasizing. Your mind is designed to create mental images.

As a child, you enjoyed inventing things in your mind, fantasizing, and pretending. As adults, we have the responsibility to dream about and focus on things we truly want to bring about in our lives, rather than just indulging in fantasies.

To begin the visualization process, become very comfortable, then create a clear picture in your mind of what you want to manifest. See it as your reality already done, as complete as possible. The more associated you can become with it, the quicker it comes into manifestation for you. So, bring the picture to life by seeing the colors associated with it, tasting anything there is to taste, feeling the textures around you, and sensing the whole energy of the environment. See yourself actively participating in this picture with the people involved and the events taking place. Breathing the feeling of this achievement into every fiber of your being, enjoy it right now using your imagination to empower your future.

The emotional impact is more important than the visualization itself. If you can feel the essence of what you want, you will manifest it. Visualization works best when you are fully engaged with what you want, incorporating all five senses. What do you hear, feel, see, smell, and taste? Carry this feeling with you into all of your daily activities.

Your brain can be a big help with this process. Have you ever bought something, only to suddenly see it everywhere? I once bought a sunshine orange Subaru Crosstrek. I thought it was unique. But as soon as I owned it, so did half the other people on the road. Where did all those bright orange Subarus come from? They were always there, but they weren't important to my brain, so they were filtered out until I made them significant to me. This filtering system is known as the reticular activating system.

"Your brain filters out what is not important to you."

There is a bundle of nerves that sits in your brain stem, and its primary function is to keep you sane and alive. It's called the reticular activating system. Every second of our lives, we are constantly bombarded with an overwhelming amount of information. Without this filtering system, we would not be able to function in this world; we would simply go insane. It keeps us focused on what's essential for our survival. If a bear were coming toward you, your reticular activating system would filter out everything else around you, so your primary focus would be on what to do about the bear.

Creative visualization enables you to program your reticular activating system by presenting it with images of the things you desire and what's important to you. When your mind constantly sees the same images, it creates a filter that shows you more of those things in your world. I did not notice so many orange cars until I got one. My filter had been shifted. If you consider yourself fat, you will automatically notice other fat people because that's important to you. If you want an electric bike, you will start to see more of them, as that's important to you.

Many people use vision boards to stimulate their reticular activating system, enabling it to generate more of those desired images in their lives. Add emotions to those images, and watch them begin to manifest in your world like magic.

Vision boards don't work by themselves; the images do nothing but make you "wish" for them. What makes it work is the energy or emotion you put into the vision. You must feel it in every fiber of your being to make it your new reality. To evoke this feeling deep within, you need to engage all of your five senses. It's easier to do so by creating a mental movie and seeing yourself as the main character.

Affirmations

The second element of VAM is affirmations. Everyone talks to themselves every day, all day long. The key is to become aware of what you're saying to yourself. Your subconscious programming is running your life, whether you're aware of it or not. It's the same mind that pumps the blood through your veins and tells your heart how many times per second to pump the blood through. You don't have to do anything consciously. Your subconscious does all the work for you to keep you alive.

It does not stop at maintaining the physical body; it also informs your world so that you may stay safe. It tells you what not to do or what you're incapable of doing, based on your past experiences or programming. It prevents you from taking risks or venturing into uncharted territory. Your subconscious mind is your inner computer, storing all the information you've acquired since birth.

"No" is such a harsh word. It instills fear and puts you on guard. At a young impressionable age, this can create a huge stop sign for you to say "yes" to the things in life that matter most. It can keep you in your comfort zone, even when it's no longer comfortable. It can prevent you from healing, from exploring life, and from being fully free and alive in your world.

As you learn to make conscious choices, you must take charge and reassure your subconscious that it's safe to take risks, venture outside your comfort zone, and grow. One way we do this is by instilling positive affirmations into our subconscious. To reprogram the subconscious takes repetition. For this reason, we recite or write out our affirmations over and over again to counter any negative mind chatter, doubt, fear, or worry about our future vision and goals.

An affirmation is a positive or negative statement you make to yourself. A negative affirmation would be, "I'm too fat." A positive affirmation would be, "I'm getting thinner and slimmer each and every day."

Writing Affirmations

1. Keep it positive.//
2. Own your affirmation by beginning the statement with "I am," or "I have," or "I am willing."
3. State it in the present tense as if it is already your reality.
4. Keep it short, sweet, and easy to remember so that it's easy to recite throughout the day.

Your inner computer (subconscious mind) is designed to bring into your experiences whatever you believe to be true. So, whatever you say is true, it is true, but only for you. Those are your thoughts, and you get to experience them out in your world. As you thinketh, so shall you become.

Using Positive Affirmations

Once you're armed with a set of positive affirmations, you can use them to counter any negative thoughts or emotions that come up during your day. If you're having a conversation with someone about losing weight, your mind might automatically go to old thoughts of how fat you feel. That would be the time to recite silently to yourself, "each and every day I get slimmer and healthier in every way."

Think about the vision you have for each area of your life and create a positive affirmation tailored to that specific area.

My affirmation for my **HEALTH** is:

_____

_____

My affirmation for my **FINANCES** is:

_____

_____

My affirmation for my **RELATIONSHIPS** is:

_____

_____

My affirmation for my **HAPPINESS** is:

_____

_____

Practicing positive affirmations will eventually shift your attitude about life as you begin to have more positive experiences. Another way to use positive affirmations is to set intentions for your daily activities. If you have a job interview, you might affirm, "I passed this interview with flying colors!" If you know you're going to need to confront someone over a particular issue, you might affirm, "My conversation with (fill in the blank) ends on a positive note for everyone." You get the idea.

Here are a few sample affirmations:

Simple affirmation for health:

Each and every day I get better in every way.

Affirmation for financial abundance:

I attract infinite abundance into my life now. Each and every day, I grow more and more abundant. I'm a money magnet. Money comes to me in ways expected and unexpected.

Affirmation for attracting a relationship.

I now attract my perfect life partner. I know that my mate is seeking me, and I need not look for him/her. I surround myself with love and receive my blessings now.

You do not need to say or remember the entire affirmation. Repeating a single line can help clear your mind of negativity and put you at ease. Now, write out one short and simple affirmation for your LIFE!

My Affirmation for My Life is (What am I affirming for my life?)

_____

_____

_____

Meditation

The last element on VAM is meditation. Meditation is a quieting of the mind. In Webster's Dictionary, the definition is "doing the wisdom." It is taking the time to be still and pray (ask) for direction and to listen (meditate) for guidance or answers.

Sitting is often considered the best position for meditation, rather than lying down, because lying down can induce a more hypnotic state, making it easier to fall asleep. A meditative state is more controlled and focused, and you can exit it more quickly and easily. In contrast, when lying down in a hypnotic state, you must return more slowly to regain total consciousness and alertness.

POSITION: Sit with your back straight to allow spinal fluid and life-force energy to flow freely up and down your spine, clearing the seven major energy centers within the body that can sometimes become blocked and cause backaches. Uncross your legs and turn the palms of your hands facing up on your thighs to be in a more open and receptive state.

PROCESS: Close your eyes and focus on the center of the forehead or the heart center. Breathe slowly in to a count of 5 through your nose; hold to a count of 5; and release the breath slowly to a count of 5. Repeat this breathing exercise 6 times.

- The first 3 times focus solely on the breath going in and out, slowly relaxing your body.
- Then visualize a small sun about 7 inches above your head and feel it sending energy down through the top of your head into your body to help you relax.
- Then feel the sun's energy coming down again to push out all the negative or stagnant energy you may have been carrying around all day.
- Lastly, see this sun's energy filling you with white light (any color is fine) and know that this light is healing every cell in your body on every level, mentally, physically, and emotionally.

PROGRAM: Learn to relax your body at will by programming it with a keyword such as "relax" or "peace." After the breathing exercises, your body is relaxed. This is the time to repeat your keyword over and over again. Then you will soon find that you do not need to do the breathing exercises to relax; you will only need to say your keyword 2 or 3 times, and your body will respond. You automatically breathe more deeply when your body is relaxed.

Here's a guided meditation to help you get started. Begin by getting clear about the guidance you wish to receive, and keep your journal nearby to jot down notes.

Go into meditation by closing your eyes and focusing inward. Breathe in to a count of 5, hold to a count of 5, and release slowly to a count of 5. Repeat the breathing exercise 2-3 more times to get fully relaxed.

Guided Meditation:

Begin to visualize the change you want as already accomplished. Get a super clear picture of what your life looks like with your desired changes in place. Create a mental movie.

See it in full color, vibrant. Breathe deeply, breathe life into it. Declare your future now. You are in charge of creating the world you wish to live in and the experiences you wish to have. Go within and create the transformation you desire.

Now, ASK, "What do I need to do to have my dreams fully realized? What is my next step?" Then BE STILL and LISTEN inward. Allow any outside sounds to just take you deeper into listening to that still small voice within. You may receive a single word, a thought, or an idea. You may get images. You may receive information that you don't think relates to your question; just trust the process.

Do this meditation every day. Meditate on your mental movie, then journal your thoughts and ideas. Journaling is one of the greatest transformational tools you can have for several reasons:

- Writing can be very therapeutic, so it's like free therapy.

- It forces you to focus on your thoughts and slow down the monkey mind, so you get clear.
- It helps you manage anxiety and reduces stress.
- It can help you cope with depression.
- It's like a track record of your personal growth and can show you how far you've come.

You can create an online journal; however, there's something special about putting pen to paper. Also, you don't have to worry about keeping it safe from peering eyes online. I suggest you purchase a journal that feels good to you and a pen that feels good in your hand. If your writing tools feel inviting to you, it will make it easier to begin journaling.

Commitment requires practice, so decide on a time and place for your writing. I suggest journaling immediately after your meditation practice, as you will already be in a comfortable and quiet space.

If you are new to journaling, start by asking yourself how you're feeling in the moment, then write down your thoughts and feelings. If you have just finished meditating, write down any guidance or insight you may have received. Don't judge anything! Just write!

Building a strong foundation for mastering your life can be done by:

- Discovering your purpose by knowing what brings you joy,
- Having a vision for specific areas of your life,
- Setting smart goals, and
- Utilizing the Power of VAM to stay the course.

Once you are on track, the object is to maintain your flow by managing your mindset and emotions. So, let's proceed to step two, "Mindset," in the "**Five Steps to Joy.**"

STEP 2 – MINDSET

The most important gift you can give yourself is the gift of Inner Peace.

Step Two – Mindset. If your mind is not at peace, you will struggle with every attempt to find happiness.

From my book *Living Inner Peace: A Personal Guide to Greater Happiness:* "Inner Peace is a sense of well-being, a sacred space you dwell deep inside yourself, where you are so connected with your creator that nothing outside of you can move you."

Inner Peace is the ultimate healing and sense of well-being that leads to happiness, joy, and fulfillment.

To achieve inner peace, we must take full responsibility for our life's experiences: We've all been hurt; we've all hurt others. We need to let go of the past and take steps to break the cycle.

Another step towards a greater sense of inner peace is to discover our sense of belonging. Everyone has a need to belong. Children who grow up in a dysfunctional home are more likely to join a gang than those who grow up in more cohesive environments. As adults, many tend to gravitate towards a church or spiritual community. Find your tribe.

Mastering inner peace means achieving balance in all areas of your life: physically, mentally, emotionally, and spiritually.

We live in a world of distractions. You may know your Soul's desires and be on a mission to fulfill your purpose, but life happens. There are ups and downs, roadblocks, setbacks, curveballs, etc. People start telling you that you can't do what you're setting out to accomplish. So-called misfortunes happen in life. To stay true to your purpose and reason for being, know that EVERY PERSON and EVERYTHING IS A BLESSING. All that is happening in your world is a result of your consciousness. If you didn't need the experience, it wouldn't be YOUR experience. So be thankful for everything that comes your way.

The actor, Jamie Foxx, suffered a stroke, and during his comeback performance, the most powerful thing he said was, "God blessed me with a stroke." He was fully aware that it happened for his highest good, and he received his blessings.

"Nothing Happens TO you - Everything Happens FOR you."

Nothing happens "to you." Everything happens "for you." When you get this mindset, you will stop fearing the unknown, worry less, and have more faith in the process of life. As a student of Life Mastery, when life happens, you will use the tools learned in this book to get grounded in the truth of your being and back on track with your Soul's desires. Here's a little prayer to strengthen your faith.

Prayer for Faith

"My mind is connected to the mind of God. Every thought I think is healing and revealing. From this day forward, I fully and completely trust the process of life. I trust that I am divinely guided, and that I am a healing force on the planet, and everyone around me is touched and moved in the most divine ways. I am open to receiving; therefore, all my needs are met at all times. All that I desire desires me. Miracles happen in my world moment-to-moment. My life is a demonstration of heaven on earth right now. I have total and complete faith that all my decisions lead me to a place of wholeness, healing, abundance, JOY, and peace of mind."

Breathe this prayer in deeply, into every fiber of your being. Breathe this into your bones, feel your skin come alive with "yes." Just say yes to knowing you are divinely guided, and all is well in your world. Yes. Life is good. Yes. All is well. Yes. Breathe.

When you walk in faith, it helps to cultivate an attitude of gratitude. Manage your mind by adopting an attitude of GRATITUDE. Live in a constant state of GRATITUDE. Be grateful for what is, what was, and whatever is to come. Remember our guiding pledge is to **"bless the past, embrace the present, and trust the future."**

"I bless the past, embrace the present, and trust the future."

Guided Process for Gratitude

Relax your body and focus on something you're most grateful for. Now let that feeling of gratitude fill your heart. Just allow yourself to feel good right now. And now, find something else to be grateful for. And allow that feeling of gratitude to fill your heart. Then find one more thing to be grateful for and allow that energy of gratitude to come into your heart and fill you up.

Now imagine that the energy of gratitude has a color, and it's your favorite color. See your heart filled with that radiant color. Notice how this color and love energy overflows, just pouring forth from your heart out into the world.

Think of all the people in your life and all the situations in your life, the good and even those that appear not so good. Take a deep breath in and release this vibrant color of gratitude from your heart into every situation and every person in your life. Just allow yourself to be grateful for what is right now, without judgment; allow it to be, because you say it is so.

If any resistance appears, acknowledge that you are grateful for it as well and allow it to pass as you continue to pour out gratitude to all that is in your life. Notice that when your life is filled with gratitude, there is no room for anything other than inner peace. Enjoy this sense of inner peace and know that you can have it at any time, at any moment, by filling your heart with gratitude and allowing it to pour over your life. Take a deep breath in, release it, and know that you can always have this inner peace; it's your choice.

Having more faith and gratitude in your life will certainly help to cultivate a greater sense of inner peace and help you to relax more about your life. Everyone has the "monkey mind." I call it the "itty bitty committee" that is constantly speaking in the back of your mind, trying to disrupt your inner peace.

Managing Your Mind

To manage your mind is to release negative thoughts, limiting thinking, tolerations, self-judgments, and judgments of others and events. Start by answering the following questions:

Negative Thoughts: What are the negative thoughts about myself that I need to release to clear my mind - thoughts that do not serve me but are constantly in my head?

_____
_____
_____

Assignment: In your journal, for every negative thought, create a positive affirmation and recite it daily until you notice the thought has disappeared from your mind.

Limited Thinking: What is the limited thinking I'm having around achieving my dreams or desires that I need to shift or transform to experience more joy in my life?

_____
_____
_____

Assignment: In your journal, for every limiting thought, create a positive affirmation, and again, recite it daily until the energy behind the thought no longer has power over you.

Tolerations: What am I tolerating, not releasing, or not accepting, that could be interfering with experiencing the fullness of my joy?

_____
_____
_____

Assignment: In your journal, make a list of the things you are tolerating in life. For each item, decide if you can do something about it. If so, set a goal to create the change. If you can't do anything to change it, create a positive affirmation to help you accept it. Acceptance will set you free.

Judgements: What are my thoughts and/or feelings about others who are living their dreams, doing what I want to do, or should be doing, with my life?

_____
_____
_____

Assignment: In your journal, write a letter to those who have what you want and thank them for showing you what is possible. Be grateful for your pathfinders.

Remember, you need to manage both your mindset and your emotional feelings to stay the course. So let's proceed to step three, "Emotions," in the "**Five Steps to Joy.**"

"In the midst of movement and chaos, keep stillness inside of you."

— *Deepak Chopra.*

STEP 3 – EMOTIONS
Managing Your Emotions

Step Three – Emotions. To allow the FULLNESS of JOY to be expressed through you, you must allow JOY to become your natural state of being in the world. Give yourself permission to live in a state of eternal JOY, regardless of circumstances. This is not to say that you deny feelings of sadness or grief when life goes sideways. You feel the feelings, but you don't let them define you. You don't allow your feelings to keep you down. You learn to manage your emotions by knowing the truth of your Soul's desires. As cold as it sounds, regardless, life goes on, and when you're on a mission to express the fullness of joy based on your Soul's desires, you pause for what your mind, body, and emotions need at the time to reflect, restore, heal, and then you move on. You keep moving forward. This is Life Mastery.

"Emotional freedom is the willingness to accept the unacceptable."

You manage your emotions by continuing to remind yourself that LOVE is the answer. There is only love, and everything is either an act of love or a cry for love. In every situation, ask, "What would love do here?"

Ask, "What would love do here?"

Manage Your Emotions

You manage your emotions by releasing negative stories from the past and the fear of the future, while practicing eternal forgiveness and unconditional love.

Fear of the Future: What if all my dreams come true? Who will be affected? How will everyone around me be affected? How will my life change? What is my biggest fear?

_____
_____
_____
_____

Assignment: Acknowledge your biggest fear and write in your journal the perfect ending to the new story you are creating.

Negative Stories: Who broke my heart, hurt me, or betrayed me? What are the major stories of my past preventing me from moving forward, not living my dreams of today?

_____
_____
_____

Assignment: In your journal, rewrite the negative stories, changing the outcome to support your dreams. Use the power of your imagination! This exercise helps to reset your nervous system to a brighter future.

Eternal Forgiveness: Emotional freedom is not holding grudges. Free up your emotional energy and open your heart by forgiving everyone for everything. Ask," Who am I carrying that's preventing me from experiencing the fullness of my joy?"

_____
_____
_____

Assignment: Silently say to each person, "I forgive you, I forgive me, and I forgive the situation. Thank you for the lessons I've learned.

Unconditional Love: I realize everyone is doing the best they can with what they have been given. Where in my life, or with whom, do I need to have more compassion?

_____
_____
_____
_____

Assignment: Let go of your need to understand the person or situation and allow yourself to have compassion. Just be willing to love, regardless. Love is the answer and the greatest healer of all. Lead with love.

It takes determination and consistency to manage your mind and your emotions to take charge of your life. And it gets even better—you must manage your daily actions and habits to be in harmony with your purpose.

Everything you do has consequences, good or not so good. Are your habits and daily actions supporting your dreams, your joy? Let's take a look at "Actions," step four in **"The Five Steps to Joy."**

Dear God,

Give me the wisdom to know where I can act, the strength to follow through, and the courage to keep believing that through You, all things are possible.

~ Leeann Carey

STEP 4 – ACTIONS

Step Four – Actions. Do you feel motivated? Are you feeling inspired? Do you stay up late and wake up early, ready to jump out of bed and start your day? If not, your purpose for living may not be fully revealed. Go back and revisit your purpose. If you're clear about your purpose, what's holding you back?

If you have fear about changing direction or moving forward, consider seeking spiritual guidance through prayer and meditation. Trust that you are divinely guided, and take baby steps each day toward doing the things that bring you joy. When your life is filled with joy, you will be motivated and inspired to stay up late and wake up early to start your day.

Managing Your Habits

Take control of your daily habits and actions by implementing a morning routine, inspired daily actions, and an evening reset program. Start by answering the following questions:

Old Habits: What are some old habits that I would like to transform to live a more joy-filled life?

_____
_____
_____
_____

New Habits: What are some new, more empowering habits I want to install that would support my purpose and add more joy to my life?

_____
_____
_____
_____
_____

Morning Routine: What are some basic morning habits I can adopt to inspire myself and add more joy each day?

_____
_____
_____
_____
_____

Daily Actions: What are some daily actions I can take towards fulfilling my purpose and adding more joy to the world?

_____
_____
_____
_____

Evening Reset: What can I do each evening to clear my mind and emotions and reset my energy for the following day? *(Think in terms of reflecting on your day, ways you could have done something differently, or made a difference in someone's life. You* *may want to create a task list for tomorrow, so your day is organized and inspiring.)* Ask, "What can I plan for tomorrow that would make me want to jump out of bed with gusto?"

_____
_____
_____
_____
_____
_____

Old habits are typically not easy to break. This is because habits are on autopilot, run by our subconscious programming. This is why it's challenging to stop smoking or stop overeating, etc. We must reprogram the subconscious computer, and this is where the power of VAM comes into play once again.

Once you've identified the old habits you wish to release, visualize the new habits you would like to install, create an affirmation to help shift your mindset, and meditate daily for guidance.

Create a daily action plan to support your dreams and an evening reset for complete rest and relaxation.

Fulfillment is the final step in **"The Five Steps to Joy."** This is where you allow the fullness of joy to be expressed through you, based on your Soul's desires. Let's go!

"All our dreams can come true if we have the courage to pursue them."

~ Walt Disney.

STEP 5 – FULFILLMENT

Step Five – Fulfillment. This final step is straightforward: be clear, stay focused, and take action in alignment with your Soul's desires. Begin by answering the following questions:

CLARITY: What is the gift I'm here to give to the world? Review step one on Purpose.

_____
_____
_____
_____

FOCUS: What is needed for me to start delivering my gifts (more education, skills, or experience, more confidence, more resources, partnership)?

_____
_____
_____
_____

Assignment: Set goals in your journal to get what's missing.

ACTION: What are some ways that I can start delivering my gifts to the world?

_____
_____
_____
_____

Assignment: Start with baby steps – step, step, leap!

Beyond My Calling

If you are not yet sharing your gifts with the world, start imagining yourself doing so. If you are already sharing your gifts with the world, begin to imagine yourself taking it to the next level and growing in your ability to be of service.

*Give what you came to give, do what you came to do.
This is your Soul's expression of joy,
through you, as you!*

PART II: THE LIFE MASTERY SYSTEM™

WHAT IS LIFE MASTERY

Life mastery is the ability to find and sustain peace and happiness so that the fullness of JOY can be expressed through you based on your Soul's desires.

Your Soul's desires bring you JOY. Following your JOY brings you Peace and happiness.

You have just completed the first five steps of a lifelong journey. The five steps to joy lead you on a journey through the four levels of life mastery.

1. **Level 1 is the Dreamer** - Getting what I need. The Dreamer suffers in a stuck reality. The level of consciousness is **"Asleep**."

2. **Level 2 is the Creator** - Creating what I need. The Creator creates change and makes things happen. The level of consciousness is "**Eyes Opened**."

3. **Level 3 is the Seeker** - Receiving what I need. The Seeker knows and looks for a better way. The level of consciousness is "**Aware**."

4. **Level 4 is the Servant** - Giving what *is* needed. The Servant walks the path of surrender and leads a joy-filled life. The level of consciousness is "**Fully Awake**."

Life mastery is not a destination; it's a journey. This system is designed to act as your personal guide, helping you stay the course and keep moving forward —from sleepwalking through life to becoming fully awake and living a happy, joy-filled life.

What Is Your Current Level of Operation

4 LEVEL OF MASTERY	LEVEL OF OPERATION	CURRENT MINDSET	EMOTIONAL AWARENESS	PHYSICAL ACTIONS	LIFE'S EXPERIENCES
1-DREAMER	Surviving	Victimhood	Fearful	Procrastination	Mis-takes
2-CREATOR	Stable	Controlling	Stressed	Determined	Difficult
3-SEEKER	Successful	Peaceful	Trusting	Empowered	Easy
4-SERVANT	Surrendered	Calm	Open	Inspired	JOYFUL

Start where you are and take the journey to level up. You may be a dreamer on some level, but a seeker on another. Everyone is at different levels of operation, and each person's journey of awakening is unique to them. However, each person must lay a solid foundation, and that starts with what brings you joy, your purpose, and your reason for living.

The first five steps of this journey cannot be overlooked.

1. **Purpose.** You need a purpose/reason for living. What brings you joy and feeds your Soul?

2. **Mindset.** You need a mindset that supports your purpose. Transform **limiting beliefs** into a positive outlook on life.

3. **Emotions.** Your emotions need to align with your Mindset. Eliminate any **emotional baggage**.

4. **Actions.** You need to behave in ways that honor your values and advance your joy. Exchange **unhealthy habits** for inspired actions.

5. **Fulfillment.** You need a way to fulfill your purpose (mission) and express your joy in the world.

With a solid foundation in place, you can begin to work the Life Mastery System™ and start the journey of awaking. Work the system daily until joy becomes your natural way of life.

The Life Mastery System™ Outlined

1. **Morning Gratitude:** List two things you're grateful for.

2. **Morning Prayer:** *"Dear God, what is the most significant way for me to express my Soul's desires and extend my JOY to be shared with others?"*

3. **Moring Meditation:** Listen in stillness for at least 15 minutes.

4. **Journaling:** Note your thoughts, feelings, ideas, and images.

5. **Manage Your Mind:** Ask, *"What one restricting thought am I harboring? Where must I have more gratitude?"*

6. **Manage Your Emotions:** Ask, *"What one thing am I holding in my heart that I need to transcend? Where must I shine more love?"*

7. **Embody Change:** Imagine yourself living the life of your dreams, giving the gifts you came here to give.

DAILY PRACTICE SHEET

(Make copies of this page or use your journal.)

Today's Date: _____

1. **Morning Gratitude:** Write down one or two things that you are grateful for. Be especially grateful for anything that seems to be going "wrong." Remember, everything is a blessing, and acceptance will set you free.

   _____
   _____
   _____

2. **Morning Prayer**: *"Dear God, what is the most significant way for me to express my Soul's desire and extend my joy to be shared with others?"*

3. **Morning Meditation:** Be still and listen for guidance. Meditate for at least 15 minutes.

4. **Journal:** Write down what came through your meditation (thoughts, ideas, feelings, images).

   _____
   _____
   _____

5. **Manage Your Mind:** Release limited thinking. Ask, *"What one restricting thought am I harboring **today** that I need to transcend to experience more joy and abundance?"*

   _____
   _____
   _____

6. **Manage Your Emotions:** Release the past. Live in the "now" moment. Your feelings today are creating your tomorrows. Ask, *"What one thing am I holding in my heart **today** that I need to transcend to be more loving, giving, and compassionate towards myself and others?"*

   _____
   _____
   _____

7. **Embody Change**. Begin to "FEEL" yourself living the life that brings more joy.

   Close your eyes and imagine what it must feel like to know your true purpose and have the fullness of joy being expressed through you, as you, based on your Soul's desires. Feel the energy swirling around you, vibrating throughout your being, requalifying your energy as you step into alignment with the new you, capable of being more, doing more, and having more to share with others. As you allow yourself to feel comfortable and confident in this energy, you begin to more fully embody the changes that are taking place in your life each and every day.

   Each time you close your eyes and imagine what the future feels like, know and declare, *"I am safe, it is ALREADY DONE!"*

WEEKLY TRACKING
7 KPI's (Key Performance Indicators)

Make 4 Copies of this page and give yourself a "YES" for each day you practice the Life Mastery System™ for personal accountability. This measures your progress for 90 days.

Week 1	Sun	Mon	Tues	Wed	Thurs	Frid	Sat
Gratitude							
Prayer							
Meditation							
Journaling							
Mind							
Emotions							
Change							

Week 2	Sun	Mon	Tues	Wed	Thurs	Frid	Sat
Gratitude							
Prayer							
Meditation							
Journaling							
Mind							
Emotions							
Change							

Week 3	Sun	Mon	Tues	Wed	Thurs	Frid	Sat
Gratitude							
Prayer							
Meditation							
Journaling							
Mind							
Emotions							
Change							

The 2-Min Check-In

Practice this for 30 days, then use this tool whenever you feel stressed. Set an alarm once an hour to ask yourself these questions

1. **MINDSET: What am I thinking about right now?** Are the thoughts I'm having keeping me in alignment with my JOY, or distracting me from my JOY? What is my level of gratitude right now for what is going on?

2. **EMOTIONS: What am I feeling right now?** Are my feelings feeding my JOY, or restricting my JOY? What is my level of love right now for what is going on?

SUSTAINABILITY
Sustaining Peace and Happiness

Life presents challenges, and we can sustain our peace and happiness by accessing our Calm during the storms of life. This can be done by amplifying our peace of mind, elevating our level of happiness, and connecting with our Soul for a deeper sense of joy. We can stay grounded and focused during challenging times by speaking the language of our Soul.

The three levels of sustainability are peace, happiness, and joy. There are times when you need to feel peace. There are other times when you want to feel uplifted and happy. Then there are times when you need a deep sense of soul connection—you want joy.

Tapping into your past experiences can bring back those feelings of peace, happiness, and joy. We achieve this through conscious recall, identifying a specific song, symbol, and/or sensation that instantly transports you to that mental and emotional state.

When going through a tough time, you get to decide how to respond by speaking the language of your soul. Be prepared in advance by knowing your symbol, song, and sensation for each of the three levels before you need to access them.

Peace: What symbol do you see that makes you feel peaceful inside? What song do you hear that calms you down? What sensations make you feel safe?

- Symbol: _____
- Song: _____
- Sensation: _____

Beyond My Calling

My Personal System:
- ○ *Symbol: Meditating Buddhas (I have them everywhere in my home)*
- ○ *Song: "Wind Beneath My Wings" by Bette Midler (calms me right down whenever I hear it)*
- ○ *Sensation: Hugs, cuddling (really brings me a sense of peace and safety.)*

Happiness: What symbol makes you smile inside, what song makes you want to dance all day, what sensation makes you feel good inside?

- Symbol: _____
- Song: _____
- Sensation: _____

My Personal System:
- ○ *Symbol: Red hearts; yellow flowers (an automatic smile comes across my face when I see these)*
- ○ *Song: "Me Too" by Meghan Trainor (I just have to dance, even if driving my car!)*
- ○ *Sensation: Dancing, laughter, playfulness, re-watching the movie "Pretty Woman" (all of these make me so very happy!)*

JOY: Joy is deeper than happiness. Joy comes from your soul. What symbol soothes your soul, what song moves you to tears when you hear it, what sensation connects you with the Divine?

- Symbol: _____
- Song: _____
- Sensation: _____

My personal system:

- *Symbol: Trees, Purple Pansy flowers or Blue-Eyed Grass (makes me think of the vastness of God)*
- *Song: "Déjà Vu" by Tenna Marie (brings tears of deep knowingness – I can relate)*
- *Sensation: Stillness, heartfelt hugs, tears of love/gratitude (soothes my soul, feels like home)*

As you evolve through time and have more life experiences, the language of your Soul may change, so be aware of what feels good and right for you to bring you more peace, happiness, and joy.

Allow Joy to become your natural way of being in the world.

Roadmap To Success

Within the four main areas of life, there are three levels of advancement:

1. Physical:
   a. **Beginner:** Health, Healing, and Well-being
   b. **Intermediate:** Environmental Health and Well-being
   c. **Advanced:** Consciously creating and manifesting life experiences

2. Mental:
   a. **Beginner:** Clarity (knowing the truth of your desires)
   b. **Intermediate:** Focus (goal setting, task, and time management)
   c. **Advanced:** Action (clear intentions and surrendered control)

3. Emotional:
   a. **Beginner:** Forgiveness of self, others, and situations
   b. **Intermediate:** Acceptance of the Unacceptable
   c. **Advanced:** Unconditional Love and Eternal Forgiveness

4. Spiritual:
   a. **Beginner** (by me): Power of VAM: Creative Visualization, Positive Affirmations, and Meditation for Beginners.
   b. **Intermediate** (as me): Affirmative Prayer, Meditation *for* Manifestation, and Journaling for Focus.

c. **Advanced** (through me): Direct Revelation, Intuitive Guidance, and Inspired Actions.

Pray for Guidance

To master your life, you must know that there is something larger than your ego. You must believe that you are not alone and that something has your back. You can call it God, Angels, your Higher Self, Super Consciousness, Spirit Guides, Master Teachers, Universal Intelligence, or any other names you may have for that which created you. I was brought up Baptist, and I've read the Bible cover to cover twice, so even though I don't identify with any religion today, references to the Bible, as well as other spiritual teachings, may be found throughout this book.

To master life means to be in alignment with that which created your life. That alignment and connection are vital to your happiness. There's a reason that you were born, and your job here on earth is to figure out the reason and answer your Soul's Call to fulfill your purpose.

So, your prayers are not just, "help me reach my goals." Your prayers seek guidance to discover your purpose and answer your Calling. Your prayer is not, "help me pay my bills and feed my family." Your prayer is "help me find my purpose and give me the courage to answer the Call." Know that this answered prayer will lead to your bills being paid and your family being fed. This, my friend, is the only way that you will master life and find sustained peace and happiness. When you are doing what you have come here to do, the alignment with your Creator takes care of you in ways you could never imagine. Life becomes magical.

If your need for survival is dictating your goals, you should pray morning, noon, and night to find your purpose to get on the right path quickly. Because just paying the bills is not living.

Beyond My Calling

You are a child of the Most High. You were never meant to suffer or be without. Prosperity is your birthright. You were also born with free will. Which means, you have the power and the ability to block your good. We block our good when we don't know any better. If you were born into a poor family, you may not know any better. If, as a child, you were told money does not grow on trees, etc., you may not know any better. We accept the programming that is introduced to us at an early age. If you were born into a wealthy family, you may not have any idea why people are poor. So, you may have pity rather than compassion. You may even look down upon the poor.

The point is, whatever next level you are seeking in your life, you need to ask for guidance. There is no begging involved. There is no need to beg for that which has already been given. Pray to get out of the way so that you may receive your blessings.

> **Simple Prayer:** *Thank you God for opening my eyes to my purpose in life so that I might see more, be more, and do what I've come here to do.*

Whatever prayer you pray, always start with gratitude and ask to be guided. Stay prayed up. Never stop praying. Pray until the prayer prays you!

PART III: THE JOURNEY OF AWAKENING

Once you've taken the first five steps to finding your joy, you begin the journey of awakening to your Soul's desires, your true calling in life.

"We have to make the choice—every single day—to exemplify the truth, the respect, and the grace that we wish for this world."

~ Oprah Winfrey

HOW LIFE WORKS

Life Mastery is not about rushing to a finish line. It's a gentle unfolding, a sacred journey towards your greater yet to be—one moment of clarity at a time—as you remember who you are and why you are here in this precious moment in history.

> *"Nothing in life is by accident. You matter. Your timing matters."*

I was an unwanted child. My mother was only fourteen when she was forced to marry my father, a man of power in a small town. She endured his abuse in silence, saving every penny she could with the idea of eventually being able to run away.

Two children later, ages 5 and 7, she finally had stashed away enough money to catch a train from Tulsa, Oklahoma, to San Diego, California. But wait, she then found out she was pregnant again - with me. She was desperate to get away, so she tried everything she could to abort the new baby. Nothing worked.

She got through the pregnancy, and when I was about three months old, she left my two older brothers with our father, wrapped me up in a blanket, and found her way to California. She named me Wanda because she says, "It's a wonder I'm here."

Life for us was not easy, but now I see every chapter as a blessing. I understand that I had to come through my mother—a strong woman—and my father—a powerful man—to become the woman I am today. There truly are no accidents.

Like you, I came for a reason. One of mine is to walk through the fire, emerge whole, and guide other women through their own storms. Along the way, I discovered a powerful truth: life is energy, and energy is everything.

> *"Everything is energy, vibrating at different frequencies."*

Everything is energy, vibrating at different frequencies. Lower vibrations feel heavy, dense, and limiting. Higher vibrations feel light, expansive, and connected. We live in a vast sea of consciousness—Spirit—ever flowing, ever seeking to experience and express itself through every living thing. Spirit desires to know itself more fully, through you, through me, through all creation.

Within this sea of energy, nothing is ever truly "new," yet everything is constantly changing. And we get to choose how we navigate these waters. Flow with the current, and life carries you. Resist it, and you feel the struggle. That is life's only real lesson—alignment brings ease, resistance creates pain.

> *"Alignment brings ease, resistance creates pain."*

We long to believe in a force outside of ourselves that cares for us, loves us, and keeps us safe. And while there is such a force, the surprising truth is—it's not only outside of you, but also within you. It is the essence of your very being. As you recognize this as your wholeness, nothing needs fixing or saving. At your core, you are already whole. You are already perfect.

So, what's the point of it all? The fact is, Spirit is experiencing itself through you. By choosing to take on physical form, we agreed to abide by both spiritual and physical laws. And while this

Life Mastery

world of matter is not our eternal home, it is our playground for now—a place to explore, create, and express in ways only a physical life allows.

To do this, we are given four sacred "bodies":

1. A Physical Body – to move, act, and touch the tangible world.
2. An Emotional Body – to feel passion, the bridge that brings Spirit into matter.
3. A Mental Body – to dream, plan, and shape those passions into reality.
4. A Spiritual Body – to keep us connected to the infinite, to remind us we are one with all that is.

When you understand this, you realize... You've already succeeded, simply by showing up.

Exercise

Take a quiet moment, breathe deeply, and reflect on the following questions. Write freely. Let your words flow without judgment. Your Soul already knows the answers.

1. What do you believe is one reason you are here, at this exact time and place?

_____
_____
_____
_____

2. How have your life experiences—both joyful and painful—shaped the person you are today?

_____
_____
_____
_____

3. Where in your life do you feel most "in the flow," and where do you feel the most resistance?

_____
_____
_____
_____

4. If you were to embrace the truth that you are already whole, how might you live differently starting today?

_____
_____
_____
_____
_____
_____
_____
_____

"Life Mastery is finding and sustaining peace and happiness to allow the fullness of joy to be expressed through you, as you, based on your Soul's desires."

Pure JOY comes from an alignment of the head and the heart, the mind and the emotions. When you are aligned, you can hear the soft, soothing voice of your Soul. You get a clear sense of what you're supposed to do. Guidance is always available to you. JOY is an overall state of well-being, beyond happiness. Happiness is dependent on external factors, whereas JOY is an internal condition created by the alignment of your head and heart.

JOY is an internal condition created by the alignment of your head and heart.

There is an energy, a power point, between the heart and the head, it's the throat center. When the heart and head are aligned, the energy culminates at the throat for expression out into the world. When you can articulate to the world your Soul's desires, the world will shift into alignment to assist you in your mission. Everything becomes effortless, life becomes easy and magical.

Your Mission in Life

Do not seek to find your mission. Let your mission find you! Your job is to do what brings you JOY. Happiness is dependent upon outside stimuli. When that stimulus dissipates, happiness turns into sadness. JOY, on the other hand, is an internal expression of the Soul. When your Soul is satisfied, you experience JOY. Extended periods of JOY turn into bliss. When you are not feeling joy, it's a sign that you are not aligned with your head and heart, and not on your path. Your unique path always leads to joy, the fulfillment of the Soul. During times of loss and grief, you will have sadness that comes and goes, but there will always be an underlying sense of deep joy and gratitude for what is, what was, and what is to come. This is life mastery.

> *There will always be an underlying sense of deep joy and gratitude for what is, what was, and what is to come. This is life mastery.*

Your mission unfolds automatically as you fulfill your Soul's desires. You may be teaching children in a classroom for one year, and the next thing you know, you're opening an orphanage in another country. When following your heart, your Soul's desires will put you on a mission in life you may never have dreamed possible.

There's always a calling from your Soul to grow, expand, and evolve. You must have the courage to answer your Soul's calling, knowing it may lead you to a very different place in life, which becomes your true purpose, the reason you are here, the reason you were born.

Your Soul is always speaking to you in that still small voice. It's always calling you deeper and deeper. You may feel called to save the children. Maybe you're called to sing, become an actor, play music, teach, heal the sick, protect the innocent, paint, serve, or sell certain products or services that you're passionate about. How you do whatever you're called to do becomes your mission and reveals your true purpose in life.

You may notice that you have a natural gift or talent that brings you JOY, and that it feels good when you share it with others. This is usually a clue as to why you're here, and it could lead you to embrace your calling systematically.

To know your Soul's desires is to become fully aware and awaken to what brings you JOY, lights you up, drives your dreams, and moves you into action each day. Your Soul is always calling you to be more, have more, and share more with the world.

Do you see Spirit as something outside of yourself that issues you a mission in life? Are you not connecting with Spirit because you fear too much would be asked of you, or you feel Spirit would require you to do something you really don't want to do? Well, this is a wake-up call. Spirit is pure energy, that endless creative stuff that always has been and always will be.

Spirit's objective is to experience itself through you, not to control you. If it wanted to control you, you would not have been born with free will. If you are waiting for Spirit to reveal your mission, you may be waiting a long time. If you are running your life in the dark, without Spirit, because you fear the light, you may struggle for a long time. If you are following Spirit around, you may be going in circles for a long time.

> *"Your mission unfolds automatically when you are expressing your Soul's desires."*

How you express yourself is your choice, a matter of your free will. Your mission is not given to you by Spirit. Perhaps that means you are responsible for creating your own mission if your life is to have purpose and meaning. Spirit's job is to support your mission so that it might have its desires met through you. How can Spirit experience itself through you if you are sitting around waiting to be struck by lightning before you act, before you express yourself, and start experiencing life? You've heard the saying "the Universe rearranges itself to fit YOUR picture of reality." Why not create a big picture, have awesome experiences, and contribute to the cosmic evolution of humankind in a big way!

Many people create mission statements for their businesses, but what about their lives? Take control of your life. Turn to Spirit (that sea of consciousness which knows all) when you feel lost or confused, but don't wait for Spirit to lead the way. Your birthright is that of choice. Spirit would never rob you of this God given birthright. Like it or not, your life is your choice. Wake up! Find out what you're good at, what brings you the most JOY, and share your JOY with the world! Live your dreams! Take action towards your dreams and trust the universe to support you in accomplishing your mission with grace and ease.

There is often a burning fire—a spiral of energy I call passion—that lies dormant within us because of the fear of moving forward.

Fear acts much like a thermostat, keeping things in balance according to the standard of acceptance we have set for ourselves. It works incredibly well, keeping us within our comfort zones. When the heat is turned down too low, something inside kicks into gear, and we take action because we become too uncomfortable or unhappy. When the heat gets turned up too high, we start pulling back because again, we become too uncomfortable. Fear lives just outside of our comfort zones, ready to jump in at the first threat of change. Fear's job is to keep us safe. Are you willing to exchange safety for the opportunity to really start living your dreams?

I ask you, what if the fire of passion rises to its peak and explodes, blowing your mind! YES! Take the risk and see what happens. Live a little, or a lot! Set the fire free and let it rise within you, showering you with its gifts.

I want to emphasize the importance of each of us finding our own happiness, independent of others in our lives, so that we can live as whole and complete individuals, thus adding more power to our relationships, love to the world, and peace to the planet. SO, FREE THE FIRE AND LIVE YOUR DREAMS!

LEVEL 1 - THE DREAMER (Waking Up)

Level 1 ~ Getting What I Need

The "**Dreamer**" suffers in a stuck reality.
The level of consciousness is **Asleep.**

Symptoms of Being Asleep

- "Me" mentality *(feeling like a victim)*
- Difficult relationships *(lack of trust)*
- Motivated primarily by needs
- Looking for power outside of self
- Seeking fulfillment in possessions
- Addictive patterns and behaviors

To find the joy and happiness you seek, you must first be willing to wake up and gain a broader view of the world. It is said that people wake up when they are fed up. I hope you are motivated enough to take the necessary steps to live a full and rich life.

If you are a religious person, be sure to delve deeper into your spiritual teachings. Attend more services, get more involved in your community. Perhaps even do some community work to connect more with people. Fellowship is important to help you awaken.

Let's begin by shifting your perception.

Imagine a world ~ where you can begin again by shifting your perception to heal the past.

We have all experienced wounds in life, varying in depth and impact. These wounds leave lasting impressions on our consciousness, shaping our perceptions and, consequently, our life experiences—both positive and negative. Healing our perception of the past is essential for healing our lives and allowing new visions to emerge.

This requires courage. Often, we become so identified with our wounds that we forget we have the power to overcome them. We allow these wounds to dictate our actions and reactions, forgetting that they belong to the past and hold no power over us today. It's time to do the work required for healing by changing our perception of the past.

Think of the parable of the blind men and the elephant.

The blind man who feels a leg says the elephant is like a pillar; the one who feels the tail says the elephant is like a rope; the one who feels the trunk says the elephant is like a tree branch; the one who feels the ear says the elephant is like a hand fan; the one who feels the belly says the elephant is like a wall.

Perception is Powerful – We Only Perceive Reality from Our Limited Point of View.

Our point of view is based on our past experiences rather than future possibilities. The best way to break free from the limitations of our past is to broaden our imagination and begin to envision what we truly want from life. This is the process of waking up and realizing you're not limited to what you are currently experiencing. You have great potential if you would dare to see it!

To expand your imagination, I refer you back to the first step of "The Five Steps to Joy," Purpose, and the "Power of VAM (visualization, affirmations, and meditation)." Visualization is one of your greatest tools for reprogramming the subconscious mind.

Your subconscious mind shapes your life's experiences by processing and storing data from past events and influences. It uses this information to keep you safe, often confining you to your comfort zone, even when it's no longer comfortable. To master your life, you must reprogram both your conscious and subconscious minds, updating them with data that empowers you to break free from self-imposed limitations.

The conscious mind is logical and thinks in "words." So, whatever you are telling yourself as true is true for you. To reprogram the conscious mind, we use positive affirmations.

In contrast, the subconscious mind is creative and processes thoughts in images. These mental pictures shape the reality you envision for yourself. Consistently visualizing negative scenarios can lead to negative outcomes in your life. To reprogram the subconscious mind, use positive imagery. Many people use vision boards and repeatedly visualize a positive mental movie to effect positive change.

Integrating positive affirmations with creative visualization cultivates the confidence to know that your desires are manifesting in the present moment. If you add your meditation practice by taking time daily to sit in stillness and ask for guidance, you will witness your world begin to shift in beautiful, magical ways. This is the Power of VAM! USE IT!!!

The way you see your past significantly influences how you feel about yourself and your future. To truly master your life, you need to feel worthy of the things you desire. Many people don't feel deserving of their good because of guilt or shame from past events. Let's clear this up right now.

Eternal Forgiveness

Life mastery is about taking back your power from the past and taking ownership of your life. The only way to take back your power is to be willing to take responsibility for your past experiences. This does not mean you created everything that has happened to you, but it does mean that you played a part.

Believe it or not, for everything that you've gone through, on some level, you signed up for it and agreed to it. If you are not ready to accept this simple truth, you are not ready to awaken from the dream state. And that's okay as well. Come back to these teachings whenever you're ready to accept the unacceptable.

You were born with a purpose —one you agreed to before you were incarnated. Your purpose is the job assignment you accepted during your term here on earth. To fulfill the assignment, you will need some experience. The Universe is designed to provide you with the experience necessary for you to fulfill your assignment.

No one ever succeeds alone. You need others to help you do your job. Those folks have also agreed to fulfill specific assignments. Some of those assignments appear to be violent and vicious, while others seem kind and loving. All of it makes up the whole. We live in a world of duality, where opposites are a vital part of humanity. Once you realize this, you will stop fighting what IS and blaming what WAS.

If your assignment is to do good, there must be a force of evil present for good to matter. Evil is only "live" spelled backwards. You also must realize that we live in a world of illusions. There is nothing real here but our thoughts that make it so. We have all agreed to pretend that a table is a table, a bed is a bed, a bad guy is a bad guy, and an angel is an angel. These are all man-made concepts that we've agreed upon and abide by.

We don't have the whole picture of reality. We only know what we learn from more evolved master teachers, such as Jesus, who was tapped into the universal wisdom of the ages. Jesus was not the only Master Teacher; there were teachers before him and after him, and there will be more teachers to come. Be willing to open your eyes, as you may be the next messiah.

I believe that radical forgiveness is essential for those who think they are victims. For those who know the truth that you signed up for what has happened, forgiveness is no longer necessary. You realize those involved play a major role in your reason for being, your purpose in life. And, if those were difficult roles to play, it's even more important for you to know within your soul that compassion is in order, not blame. Not everyone gets to play the good guy. It takes courage to sign up for the role of the villain.

Learn to practice what I call eternal forgiveness. On a human level, there will be things said and done that hurt or offend you. It's not that person's fault. Whatever came your way was meant for you to help you grow. As you continue to practice eternal forgiveness, you will notice there are fewer and fewer instances where you feel the need to forgive anyone for anything. You stop attracting those types of situations because you've surrendered blame. You've taken responsibility for your assignment here on earth. You know it's all a part of growing into your full potential to serve your purpose and embrace your calling. The longer you hold on to grudges, the more they zap your power to be creative and shift from surviving to thriving.

Releasing Past Grudges

Name who hurt you most? _____

Who else hurt you? _____

Who else hurt you? _____

Who else hurt you? _____

There may be more people or situations that have caused you pain, and you can write them all out in your journal. Once you've completed your list, find a quiet place and get comfortable. Place your hands over your heart, which signifies opening your heart. Take the time with each person or situation on your list and make the following statements:

I forgive you because I now realize it was a necessary part of my growth experience.

I thank you for helping me grow, and I'm choosing to become stronger because of it.

I release you because I need to free myself of the negativity I've been carrying around.

I bless you on your journey that you may find peace and serenity, knowing all is well.

The first step is to acknowledge any grudges you may be holding onto from your past and release them. The second step is to realize incidents that show up in your future are just showing you where you need to stop blaming life and start embracing truth.

"Stop blaming life and start embracing truth."

Healing the Inner Child

A significant portion of the work we need to do regarding forgiveness stems from our childhood. Most parents do the best they can with what they were given. Years ago, I attended a talk about post-traumatic slave syndrome given by Dr. Joy DeGruy.

Her research explains many of the survival behaviors of African Americans today. Here are a few facts I found interesting about how our upbringing may affect us.

Self-Esteem: During slavery times, White women bragged about their children when they were doing well. When a Black woman received a compliment about her child, she would immediately put the child down by saying something like, he/she is lazy and does not behave well." Black women learned that the "good" kids were taken away from them and sold. Therefore, to protect their children, they would make comments about how lazy they were, etc. So many Black children may have suffered from lower self-esteem as they did not receive a lot of positive reinforcement like White children.

Taking Risks: If a White woman were standing in line at a bank with her little children, they would be permitted to run all over the place, touching things and climbing upon them, exploring! If a Black woman is standing in the same line with her little children, they are clinging to her skirt. They have been taught and programmed to stay close for safety. If a child did try to stray when the mother was not looking, and another Black mother saw this, she would immediately tell that child to get back to their mother. It goes deep! So Black children were not permitted to run free, explore, and take risks like White children.

One more thing I found interesting in Dr. DeGruy's talk was about the sense of urgency between cultures. In the European climate, you have 3 months to plant your crops to survive. The entire concept of survival revolves around timing. In the African climate, you have 9 months to plant your crops, so you can relax. In an office setting, the White boss walks in and wonders why his African American workers are standing around the coffee station exchanging pleasantries when there's work to be done! It's in our

DNA to be serious and on time, or we are on "African time." "Don't worry, be happy."

So, we are not only a product of our parents' upbringing, but also their parents' and their parents', whether good or bad, positive or negative. The good news is that because we are awake and aware of the influences we've encountered, we have the choice to shift the dynamic within ourselves and grow beyond our past. We can begin to set a new direction for ourselves and for future generations.

The point is that our childhood affects our adulthood until we make a conscious decision to change it.

> *"What we are not changing, we are choosing."*

A variety of inner child work therapies are offered by therapists and some life coaches today. I view this in the same way I view forgiveness; it's not necessary when we know the truth and are willing to integrate the lessons and blessings.

As an NLP (neuro-linguistic programming) practitioner, we work with "parts" of us, and one of the parts is the inner child. It is believed that there are certain parts of us that, due to an impactful event, stopped growing, or simply rebel against reaching our full potential.

Except for a few powerful NLP processes, I've essentially set aside many of my NLP tools, because when you see the whole picture and walk in truth, there is no need to process all these parts. It's easier and more graceful to set an intention and know that all parts of you are in alignment with your purpose and mission in life. When you state such a command with conviction (knowingness), it is done unto you as you believe.

Affirmation for Aligning the Inner Child

All parts of me are in perfect alignment and supporting me in fulfilling my life's purpose with grace and ease.

Whenever you feel like you're procrastinating or self-sabotage is at play, recite this affirmation with total conviction. Command all parts of you to shift into alignment with your higher good. It's as simple as commanding your hand to scratch an itch. You just will your hand to the area of the itch and scratch without any further thought. Command your inner child to get on board with your purpose, regardless of past experiences. Be willing to let go of the past.

A Deeper Forgiveness Process

Did you do the written process for releasing grudges? Well, this process takes things a little deeper.

Imagine you are standing before a closed elevator door. The door opens, and it is beautifully decorated. It is quite spacious, featuring two chairs and a small table adorned with freshly cut flowers. There is plush carpeting on the floor and an exquisite nature scene hanging on the side wall. You also notice that the back of the elevator has doors that also open.

You walk in and take a seat. The doors close, and the elevator begins to rise to the next level. The front elevator doors open and standing there is the person you need to forgive most. You invite them in to have a seat. They enter, and the doors close. You begin to have a conversation, one that you don't consciously need to remember, as the sound of the elevator moving drowns out the voices. You just sense that this is a very healing and gratifying conversation.

When the elevator reaches the next level, the back doors open, and that person steps out. The back doors close, and then the front doors open. Standing there is the next person you most need to forgive. You invite them in to have a seat. They enter, the doors close, and the elevator begins to rise to the next level, allowing you to have a very deep and healing conversation with this person. The elevator's noise drowns out the sound, but you can feel and sense that all is well and forgiven by the time it reaches its next level and stops.

The back doors open, and the person exits. The doors close, then the front doors open once again. And, again, standing there is yet another person you most need to forgive. You invite them in to have a seat. They enter, the doors close, and the elevator begins to rise to the next level as you have your conversation. The elevator reaches the next level, the back doors open, and the person exits.

You realize there may be more people waiting to spend time with you. However, you decide to take a break and will come back to this process later if needed. You now find yourself back in your room feeling lighter, alive, more integrated, and freer.

Your Assignment

Realize that each person has given you a gift through the experience that hurt you, and that you have given each person a gift as well.

True forgiveness is when you can say,
"Thank you."

True forgiveness is when you can say, "thank you." Fill in the blanks for each person on your list.

1. Person's Name: _____
2. I forgive you for _____
3. and I thank you for _____

Example: Jim, I forgive you for crashing my car, and I thank you for reminding me that the value of our relationships is more important than our possessions.

When we think of the pain we are in, or the pain we have suffered, it's difficult to remember that we signed up for all of this, and there are no accidents in God. There is nothing new under the sun. The alpha and the omega, the beginning and the end, are one. God created you; God sustains you, and you are an individualized expression of the one God. There is no place where God is absent. Every situation is designed to beckon us to the highest degree of human potential, our calling, our reason for incarnation.

Don Miguel Ruiz wrote the book, "The Four Agreements." When we learn to live by these simple rules, we encounter less pain and more joy.

The Four Agreements *by Don Miguel Ruiz*

1. **Be impeccable with your word.** Speak with integrity. Say only what you mean. Avoid using your words to speak against yourself or gossip about others.

2. **Don't take anything personally.** Nothing others do is because of you. What others say and do is a projection of their own reality, their own dream. When you are immune to the opinions and actions of others, you won't be the victim of needless suffering.

3. **Don't make assumptions.** Find the courage to ask questions and express what you really want. Communicate with others as clearly as you can to avoid misunderstandings, sadness, and drama. With just this one agreement, you can completely transform your life.

4. **Always do your best.** Your best is going to change from moment to moment. Under any circumstance, simply do your best, and you will avoid self-judgement, self-abuse, and regret.

These four agreements that you make with yourself may seem simple, but there is always one that is more difficult to uphold than the others. The one that's difficult for you today will get easier as time goes on and you continue practicing living by these agreements.

Don't try to force others to live by these rules, as that can create drama. Allow others to be where they are, accept them for who they are, and show them how they can grow and become different. Be the example, be the light for them.

I have found that by implementing these standards into my life, those who are not in alignment will either begin to shift and get on board, or they will be removed from my life by the Universe. I just need to stay true to myself.

Another important factor of mastering your life is managing your health. There are things within your control, and then there are things that will happen that seem out of your control. You may not be in control of your body if a bone is broken and you're in a lot of physical pain. However, you are ALWAYS in control of your mind and the thoughts you are thinking about the body's condition. When you focus on and invest energy in positive thoughts, your body heals faster because energy naturally follows the path of least resistance. So let's talk about your health.

Before we go too deep into healing, let me just say that love is the greatest healer of all.

The Enlightened Heart

The fastest way to healing is through the enlightened heart.

- Love is the most powerful force in the universe.
- The heart is the generator that pumps life force energy into the cells and throughout the body.
- The energy from the heart radiates down the arms and out of the palms of your hands for hands-on healing.

I've had the privilege of being in the presence of, and receiving hugs from Mata Amritanandamayi, a prominent Indian Hindu spiritual leader and humanitarian known as Amma (meaning "Mother"). The first time I received a hug from her, it was so powerful that the energy almost took me to my knees. It showed me just how powerful it is to be fully embraced by love.

The enlightened Heart only knows love, the highest vibration.

One of the reasons the Master Teacher Jesus was able to heal the sick was because he was pure love; he had an enlightened heart.

The Enlightened Heart transfers love energy through conscious intent.

Vibration heals. Energy vibrating at a higher frequency can override lower vibrations to create a space for healing to take place.

Illness is a misalignment of the body, and raising your vibrations puts you back in alignment.

Now, for those of us who do not yet possess an enlightened heart, let's walk through what it might take to achieve better health and healing.

Your Health

If our health is gone, we can restore it.
If our health is threatened, we can protect it.
If our health is perfect, we can preserve it.

What IS Healing?

- Physical healing is the realignment of the body with the Soul.
- The body is the vehicle by which the Soul gets to experience life.
- The Soul is your reason for being, it's your driving force for life.
- What connects body and soul is breath, life force energy.
- Healing happens through a transfer of energy. The rate of frequency causes molecules to change form.
- Energy is transferred through **thoughts, words, and/or actions**.
    - Thoughts (higher frequency). Think quantum healing.
    - Words (mid frequency).
    - Touch (lowest frequency).

- Negative thoughts and emotions can block the flow of energy and prevent healing.

Energy and Dis-Ease

Everything is energy vibrating at a certain frequency. Our physical bodies vibrate from 236 to 360 trillion times per second to remain solid. Whenever there is a health problem, there is a lack of energy circulating to that particular part of the body. There is a block in the transmission of energy to the dis-eased area.

There are seven major energy centers that move through the body. These energy centers are not located in the physical body for the physical eye to see; they are in the etheric (spiritual) body. These energy centers are known as chakras, a Sanskrit word that means "wheel" or "disk". It refers to spinning wheels of energy located along the spine. Seers throughout the ages describe them as being about 2 to 2 1/2 inches in diameter, having a distinct color, and governing various organs within the body.

Healers of various modalities understand chakras and their primary function of supplying energy directly to vital body organs. These healers will work with clients to free up any blocked energy and restore balance to the mind and body.

Chakras not only govern energy to certain body organs, but also influence certain aspects of your mental and emotional well-being.

The seven major chakras (energy centers):

1. Root Chakra

- Location: Base of the spine, dominate color is red

- Governs: Adrenal glands, bones, and the nervous system, including the lower back and legs
- Represents: Stability, survival, grounding, and physical identity
- Imbalance Signs: Issues with the colon, bladder, lower back, legs, and immune system, fear, anxiety, financial instability, feeling disconnected from your body or surroundings
- Balanced State: You feel healthy, safe, grounded, and secure.

2. Sacral Chakra

- Location: Lower abdomen, about 2 inches below the navel, dominate color is orange
- Governs: Gonads (ovaries and testes), kidneys, bladder, reproductive organs, and hips
- Represents: Creativity, sexuality, pleasure, emotions, and relationships
- Imbalance Signs: Reproductive issues, urinary problems, or lower back pain, guilt, creative block, sexual dysfunction, emotional instability
- Balanced State: You experience joy, creative flow, and healthy emotional and sexual expression.

3. Solar Plexus Chakra

- Location: Upper abdomen/stomach area, dominate color is yellow.
- Governs: Pancreas, spleen, and the digestive system, regulating blood sugar and metabolism
- Represents: Personal power, confidence, willpower, and self-discipline

- Imbalance Signs: Digestive problems, liver or gallbladder issues, diabetes, low self-esteem, and control issues
- Balanced State: You feel confident, motivated, and in control of your life.

4. Heart Chakra

- Location: Center of the chest, dominate color is green
- Governs: Thymus gland, the immune system, heart, and lungs
- Represents: Love, compassion, forgiveness, and connection
- Imbalance Signs: Asthma, high blood pressure, or heart disease, loneliness, bitterness, fear of intimacy, difficulty in relationships
- Balanced State: You feel love, empathy, and a sense of connection to others.

5. Throat Chakra

- Location: Throat, dominate color is blue.
- Governs: Thyroid and parathyroid glands, which control metabolism
- Represents: Communication, truth, expression, and integrity
- Imbalance Signs: Sore throat, thyroid problems, or neck and shoulder stiffness, fear of speaking, lying, shyness,
- Balanced State: You express yourself easily, clearly, and authentically.

6. Third Eye Chakra

- Location: Between the eyebrows, dominate color is indigo

- Governs: Pineal and pituitary glands, influencing perception and thought
- Represents: Intuition, insight, wisdom, and imagination
- Imbalance Signs: Headaches, sinus issues, vision problems, sleep disorders, poor decision-making, lack of focus, disconnection from intuition
- Balanced State: You experience mental clarity, insight, and strong intuition.

7. Crown Chakra

- Location: Top of the head, dominate color is purple, violet, or white (*for some reason, the crown chakra always appears purple for me*)
- Governs: Pineal gland, connecting to the brain and spiritual awareness
- Represents: Spiritual connection, enlightenment, and universal consciousness
- Imbalance Signs: Headaches, migraines, and nerve pain. cynicism, disconnection from spirit
- Balanced State: You feel a deep sense of peace, purpose, and oneness.

Whenever you feel ill or out of balance, you may have energy blocks. Stress is one of the biggest reasons energy stops flowing freely through your system.

When the chakras are blocked, energy does not flow freely throughout your system, resulting in discomfort, and if blocks are not removed, it can lead to dis-ease. If you feel blocked in any way, in any area, consider clearing and cleansing your energy centers.

You can read books and attend lectures that offer lengthy, sometimes complicated methods for clearing and cleansing the chakras. I believe that if it is a part of you, you can control it simply by knowing that you can and directing the flow of energy accordingly.

To clear the chakras, visualize a brilliant ball of white light, representing pure God energy, entering the top of your head and moving down through your body to the root chakra at the base of your spine. Then, as the white light enters that lower chakra, see it begin to spin the chakra (wheel of energy), opening it up. As the white light spins the chakra, it clears away any debris, cleansing that center so that energy may flow more freely. See in your mind the chakra color going from red to pink, then to white, and finally to clear.

Once that center has been cleared, focus your attention on the sacral chakra, the next one up, and repeat the same visualization technique. Bring in a ball of white light from above the top of your head down into the sacral area. Have the white light enter that chakra and start spinning it, opening it up, and spinning off all debris. See the color go from orange to white to clear.

Perform this process with each chakra, all the way up to the crown center, then expand the white light energy to encompass all areas of the body, covering all body organs.

Clearing and cleansing the chakras is needed whenever you feel a lack of energy. Sometimes you can pinpoint which part of you feels drained; other times, you may want to cleanse your entire system.

Body Maintenance

Everything you need to be whole and complete is already within you. We often underestimate the power of our own minds to heal our bodies. It is the subconscious mind's job to control our bodily functions without conscious effort. You don't need to consciously tell your heart to pump; your body has intelligence and knows how to run itself and take care of itself. When the body becomes out of balance due to an action that causes stress, it knows how to restore its balance. When the mind is at peace, the body can heal itself. Get out of the way of your own healing by letting go of all that does not serve you. Letting go of all the things in your life you are tolerating. Be at peace, be balanced (mind and soul), and you will be healthier.

To demonstrate the power of the mind, studies have shown that patients, without being told, were given candy pills as their medication, and received the same healing benefits as those who were actually receiving the medication. If you take medication, healing occurs because of your faith in the medication. If you do prayer and laying on of hands, the healing takes place because of your belief in the power of what you are doing. Either way, the healing takes place because you believe it will, because of your faith.

Another study showed a man was hypnotized and given eight glasses of Vodka and told it was eight glasses of water. After drinking eight glasses of Vodka, he showed no signs whatsoever of intoxication in his actions, and his blood/alcohol content was normal within his body. We can heal our bodies and live our dreams if we release the fears and stresses that hold us back.

Your Attitude Counts

Your attitude about your health is just as important as the energy you take in. Some people have a pattern of becoming ill to receive more attention, to be taken care of, or to justify taking time off from work or the need to pamper themselves. It is up to everyone to find their own happiness and not depend on others to take care of them. It is our duty to take care of ourselves. That means we stop when we need to stop, and we don't do disease to get permission to stop. Give yourself permission to say no, and ask for the attention you want/need, to pamper yourself, and take time off from work just because you deserve it.

Your attitude stems from your belief system. If you believe people are kinder to you when you are ill, you are more likely to become sick when you sense a confrontation is in store for you. You created such a belief, and you can always change your mind. Decide right now that people are always kind to you and enjoy you more when you are happy and healthy.

Do yourself a favor when you become ill and start asking yourself:

1. How is this illness serving me?
2. What am I getting from being ill that I would not usually get?
3. What do I need to do to get better faster?

Visualization For Health

Visualization is one of the most powerful tools for healing. If you use your phone or any method to record and play back the following guided process in your own voice, it creates an even deeper impact upon your subconscious mind.

Feel yourself becoming extremely light, begin to float and drift away, and rise higher and higher. Look into the center of the sun. See yourself drawn closer and closer to the sun until you have merged with it completely, becoming one with it. Make it a part of you; it is all energy, life force itself. You are now total energy, and you are the life force. Bath and heal yourself in this field of life force energy. See yourself now whole and complete, perfect in every way and on every level, physically, mentally, emotionally, and spiritually; fit and trim, attractive and active, outgoing and happy. Enjoy this new freedom now.

It's time to return to Earth. You will return with all the health and energy you have just experienced. Allow your experience to be your new reality; you have that power, make it real with the power of your mind. Feel the revitalizing energy of the sun renewing every cell of your body, making you whole and complete. Know that anytime you feel depleted, you need only remember this experience, and you will again instantly receive healing energy from the sun.

Coming back slowly now, ease back into your physical space and slowly bring your awareness back into the room by opening your eyes.

Affirmation For Health

I only entertain thoughts to indicate perfect balance and perfect health circulating in my life.

I know that whatever I consume is good for me and that food merely goes right through my system, leaving behind only vitamins, minerals, and other nutrients that my body chooses to use.

My body, through cellular memory, KNOWS what it needs, when it needs it, and how to get it without my help. My body is self-maintained, and I eat primarily for pleasure and the sense of taste. My body is made of the same substance as our planet Earth, and, as part of Mother Earth, the environment provides the highest-quality nourishment for my physical body. My body automatically absorbs the necessary elements through breath and the air around me, as they are filtered through my pure light consciousness, rejuvenating my entire being.

Affirmation for Becoming Whole Again

All parts of me are in perfect alignment, supporting me in fulfilling my life's purpose with grace and ease.

Notations on Health

Notations by Paul Brenner, M.D., from the book: *"Health is a Question of Balance."*

- Dis-health occurs in that millisecond that an individual puts himself/herself down for being anything less than perfect.

- Suffering has the propensity to heighten one's awareness. Do you need pain to make today count?

- What are you getting out of illness that you can't achieve in health?

- Healing requires taking responsibility. Responsibility means personal involvement in the present, not blame for the past.

- Balance is the still point of what is and what is not.

You are ready to move to the next level! You are managing your mindset and emotions by working the Life Mastery System™. You're learning to sustain peace and happiness during the storms by making "calm" your new superpower!

Life Mastery

You are awake to the possibilities. You are no longer stuck or feeling hopeless. You understand how life works, recognizing that everything is energy, which follows the path of least resistance. Therefore, you utilize the power of VAM and focus your energy on visualizing a brighter future for yourself. You focus on positive affirmations when doubt creeps in, and you meditate daily for guidance.

You've shifted your perception of the past and come to realize that everyone, including yourself, is just doing their job. Therefore, there's no need for forgiveness. You practice eternal forgiveness for everyone and everything. You practice the four agreements and live with integrity to lessen the drama of life.

You are taking charge of your physical well-being and beginning to sense when and where you feel blocked. You unwind by opening your chakras, which balances your system and allows energy to flow through you freely, returning you to peace and balance.

You walk daily with an attitude of gratitude because you've got this! You are becoming the master of your life, and you know that all is well. You've awakened to what brings you joy, and you're no longer dreaming awake; you are ready to move on to the next level and become the Creator!

Begin to Study A Course in Miracles

As an introduction to becoming the Creator, one of my favorite classic study courses for truly waking up and becoming aware is "A Course in Miracles." I highly recommend this course. There are 365 days a year, and 365 lessons in the book. You can start lesson 1 on any day of the year. It's so powerful that you will want to repeat it over and over again.

You can purchase the book or listen to the lessons on YouTube. Carol Howe has recorded all 365 lessons, and at the time of this writing, you can listen to them freely on YouTube. There's also a free PDF version of the book you can download online.

LEVEL 2 - THE CREATOR (Eyes Opened)

Level 2 ~ Creating What I Need

The "**Creator**" creates change and makes it happen! The level of consciousness is **Eyes Opened**.

Benefits of Eyes Opened and Being Awake

- You have a broader view of the world
- You understand and use Universal Laws
- You are no longer chasing your needs
- You have improved self-confidence
- You begin to heal/take care of your body
- You are fostering healthier relationships

You get to reap all the above benefits when you take charge of your life and start consciously creating your realities.

By this time, you are aware of what you want out of life, your purpose. As your mission is unfolding, you will want to step into your power by participating in the creative process. You were given free will – it's time to use it to manifest your desires.

Many people have read the book and/or seen the movie, "The Secret," which speaks to the Law of Attraction. Many have tried using the law and have failed to attract their desires, mainly because they don't understand the creative process.

Life is about taking FULL responsibility for the choices you make consciously **and** unconsciously. We are always making choices on some level. The life we are living is a result of those choices. No one is to blame for your life. Not your parents, not your teachers, not society. **Your life is built upon your choices.** How many times have you heard of or seen extraordinary individuals turn defeat into opportunity, handicaps into victories? It is not because they were smarter or more blessed than anyone else. It was simply because they decided to take responsibility for their lives and the choices they were making each day.

We are not human beings having a spiritual experience. We are spiritual beings having a human experience. So we often forget to take full responsibility for our lives. How many times have you just wanted to crawl underneath your bed and say, "Goodbye, cruel world!" This is because we forget that we are the ones in charge of our lives. Yes, you create your life moment by moment, and no one can take it away from you without your permission. And, yes, some of us love to give our power away. Stand in your power and become the empowered being you were meant to be.

It is up to each of us to take full responsibility for our own lives and give up the illusion that we are victims. When you decide that you no longer need to play a role that no longer serves your higher good, nor the higher good of humanity, you will have taken the first step toward awakening to your true spiritual connection.

Scientifically speaking, every thought carries an electrical impulse that triggers an emotional response that causes you to act or react in a certain way. Now I ask you, who is in charge of the thoughts that cause you to act or react? You can let anyone fill your head with negative thoughts, or you can take charge of your thoughts, feelings, and actions by learning to focus your attention on nurturing, supportive, and empowering experiences that support your overall well-being. This is Life Mastery!

Most people who are trying to activate the law of attraction have not taken full responsibility for their lives. They are still, on some level, blaming others for their current circumstances. This is giving your power away and diminishing your ability to manifest your desires.

Being fully responsible means owning all your experiences, the good and the not-so-good. This means that you no longer blame others for your experiences in life because you understand "***The Creative Process***." **It works even if you don't believe in it or you are not consciously aware of it**. If you are not consciously aware, the Creative Process is run by your subconscious patterns and beliefs (thoughts), and it's creating like crazy. Isn't it time you took control (responsibility) and started designing what you really want in life?

Taking responsibility means letting go of the drama that runs your life and being able to respond rather than react to life's situations. It's time to take back your power!

The Creative Process

1. We exist in a sea of energy called consciousness or Spirit.

2. Spirit strives to experience and know itself through us.

3. We are an individualized aspect of Spirit referred to as the Soul, seeking expression for the evolution of consciousness.

4. As an individualized expression of Spirit, we also have free will and choice.

5. As a product of the physical plane, we choose our life's experiences through our thoughts, feelings, and actions.

> *"We choose our life's experiences through our thoughts, feelings, and actions."*

The Creative Process in Action
(As channeled by Wanda Marie, 2007)

Energy moves through specific planes/fields of existence and through our bodies as a vehicle for expression into the world of form.

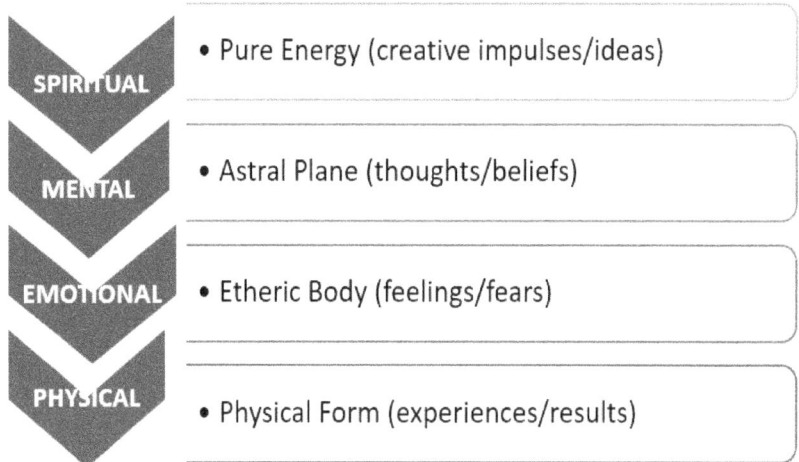

Ideas originate in the spiritual plane, a sea of energy that we all inhabit. An idea first enters the mental body, far from the physical plane (it's just an idea). There, it is judged by you, consciously or subconsciously, for logic and practicality based on past thoughts or experiences. If you buy into it —whether it's good or bad for you —like a magnet, the idea starts to attract and accumulate other ideas with similar vibrational frequencies until it becomes potent enough to become a Thought Form held within your Mental Body of desires/prayers.

The Thought Form in Action: A thought travels from the Mental Body (Astral Plane) into the Etheric Body of e-motions (energy in motion), seeking validation from your feelings (do you really want this?). If it gains enough momentum through feelings, it begins to crystallize, and a mold is created for manifestation in the physical world.

You now have a Thought Form (from the Astral Plane) set into motion through your emotions, which has created a mold for physical expression through your Etheric Body. Now, if you're intuitive or sensitive to energy, you start FEELING that SOMETHING is happening. If you are not consciously creating your world, you may not be aware of what is happening, but you can sense that something is about to shift/change.

Consciousness in Action: The Universe takes over from here to bring it into manifestation. It is as automatic and precise as the planets moving in orbit. Once that Thought Form becomes sufficiently crystallized, the energy frequency slows to the point that it is automatically propelled into physical existence and takes on physical form. This is YOUR Consciousness in action!

Manifestation: The physical plane provides the space needed for materialized objects. You must have a "space" for an object to exist in, and you must have the element of "time" to slow down energy frequency to make the object solid enough to occupy the space. The crystallized form (object) remains in existence as long as you maintain the consciousness (thought form) that holds it in place. Once you decide you no longer want/need it, it starts to dissipate. That is why it is said we live in a world of maya (illusions). When it dissipates, the energy moves from the physical plane back into the astral plane. Then it re-enters the spiritual plane, where time and space do not exist; therefore, no physical form can exist.

EVERYTHING ORIGINATES IN PURE CONSCIOUSNESS AND RETURNS TO PURE CONSCIOUSNESS. It is the consciousness within you that creates AND maintains your experiences. You create your own realities, like it or not.

Life becomes amazing when you know you can have it all because you are consciously creating your life's experiences. You feel more at peace with what you are creating for yourself. And there is more peace when you allow others to make their own choices and create their own experiences, whether good or not-so-good.

Imagine what your life would look like if you were fully surrendered to having your heart's desires, and nothing could stop you. (*Pause and take that in*). Just imagine. Imagine what your life would be like if you had all that you truly desire. (*Pause and feel that energy*). Just imagine. I'm here to tell you that you can truly have it all.

"You can truly have it all."

Your imagination is one of the most powerful tools for personal transformation. Children use it all the time. As we grow older, we start adulting and forget to allow our imagination to run wild. The following is a guided process for reconnecting with your imagination, consciously creating, and redirecting your life.

Redirecting Your Life

Imagine sitting in your own private little movie theater with a giant silver screen in front of you. This is your private screening of a film, where you get to be the star. You are the only person in the theater, and you are sitting in the director's chair. You look down and see that you have control buttons on the arm of your chair, allowing you to fast forward, pause, and rewind the film. You can even cut and edit segments right from your chair by using the delete button. You are in charge of your life. You are the creator and the director.

You press the "start" button, and the film begins to roll. You see a snapshot of yourself as an infant. You see another still frame of yourself: a toddler, a young child going to school, a teen —and now there is nothingness. The frames go blank. Whatever has happened in your past movie is done and complete. From this moment on, you get to recreate your story. You get to rewrite the script, and even if the last one was great, you get to make it even better. What are your heart's desires for your life? If you already have all that you want and need, what are your heart's desires for this world? What story will you tell that improves the quality of your life or the lives of all of humanity? What story will you tell? See the story you are creating starting to play out on the big screen. As the film rolls, find a scene in it that you cherish most and then press pause. This could be a scene where you are truly enjoying your new life, surrounded by friends, a lover, or a transformed relationship with a family member. This could be a scene of children who were once starving celebrating with a feast, while the homeless are warm and safe. Wherever the new story leads you, follow it until a scene touches your heart. Press pause and then surrender to that moment. Be present in the moment and embrace it. Know that it is real, and this is a new world you have created for yourself. Look at all the details in this frame, frozen in time. Feel that you are there now. Breathe it in and get totally comfortable with this scene. Take it deeper and deeper into your heart. Breathe it in.

Now make this picture of your new reality larger than life. Expand the image beyond the silver screen to fill the entire room, allowing it to come to life right before your very eyes with you in the center. You notice you are no longer in the director's chair; you are living your new life! You realize that something bigger than *you has taken over. You can call it your Higher Self, God, or whatever feels right for you. But you trust the director and can now go about just enjoying your new life.*

Notice how wonderful it feels to know that you've written the script; through your God given free will, and now, God's in charge as you have surrendered and gotten out of the way. There is no better director than God. Life is good, and you know this. So, you allow your subconscious mind to continue living out this scene as you bring your awareness back to your current reality. As you return your focus here, you know that once a plan has been imprinted upon the subconscious mind, it must be delivered. Therefore, what you have created is real in the mind of God and shall be made real in your world. Your only job is to stay out of the way and walk in faith. Take a deep breath in. Release and let go.

You are, and have always been, the creator of your life's experiences. As you awaken to your power of choice, you will begin to make more conscious choices.

If the idea of conscious choice and creating your own realities is new to you, you will doubt your power to do so. I ask you to begin by manifesting small things to prove to yourself just how powerful you really are. Many people start by creating parking spaces. Ask the Universe for a great parking space. It's that easy. If you don't get a great space, it's only your disbelief that short-circuits the flow. Keep asking for the perfect parking space. Soon, you'll realize you no longer have to ask; the perfect parking space always shows up for you. I personally call forth my "parking angels" to prepare a space for me as I'm arriving at my destination.

This is setting your intention—the power of intention is underestimated. Declare your power, step into it gently and lovingly – and use it wisely.

Now that you realize you are the creator of your life's experiences, what experiences will you choose for yourself, your life? What kind of life do you want to live? What kinds of experiences do you want to have?

If you decide, for the sake of collective consciousness, to experience life as a homeless person, then this becomes your reality. There is nothing good or bad about it. If, on some level, you decide to experience the death process through an accident or disease, there is nothing good or bad about it. There is no such thing as death. It is just another experience. Spirit is endless and timeless, and you, your Soul, is infinite and timeless as well.

If you decide to experience life through creating fame and wealth, there is nothing good or bad about it. If you choose to devote your entire life to worshiping God/Spirit, there is nothing bad *or good* about it. These are all only experiences.

To begin experiencing the rewards of the Creator:

1. **Get the support you need.** If you're not part of a spiritual or metaphysical group, please find one now. Don't be a lone ranger on the path. Even if you think you are doing better alone, you are not! No one does. We were built to connect with each other, to support each other, and to be companions to each other. There are tons of online groups out there waiting for you! Explore and find one that feels right for you. Get involved!

2. **Continue Positive Affirmations:** Think of positive affirmations as your daily dose of "feel good." If you don't take your medicine, it's like leaving the house without washing your face. Make prayer and affirmations a part of your morning routine to set a positive tone for your day.

3. **Use your imagination** to create an amazing feature film of your new life. Rehearse your movie every night as you drift off to sleep. Make it as real as possible by incorporating all five senses and feeling into the energy of your movie.

4. **Keep journaling** and write something every day. Think of your journal as your guiding system. Write down your meaningful activities, magic moments, fearful thoughts, insights, inspirations, awarenesses, and ideas.

5. **Practice eternal forgiveness** for everyone and everything. Remember to take full responsibility for all your life experiences. ALL OF THEM. Live in a constant state of gratitude for all that is, all that was, and all that is to come. Then watch how the magic begins to unfold in your life.

As you continue on the path, the journey deepens as you embark upon becoming the Seeker. When I learned to use my power and started creating amazing things in my life, I finally got bored. I had everything (material things), and I wanted something more. So, I wondered, what's beyond creating what you want? I was awake, and now I wanted to become aware of what else was possible.

"What's beyond the Law of Attraction is Grace."

LEVEL 3 - THE SEEKER (Aware)

Level 3 ~ Receiving What I Need

This is the "**Seeker**" who knows and looks for a better way. The level of consciousness is **Aware.**

Benefits of being aware

- All your needs are met systematically
- You realize your dreams are coming true
- You see an increase in your finances and have a greater sense of overall prosperity
- You have more peace and less stress as you allow people their truth and no longer argue
- You enjoy spreading love whenever you go
- You enjoy healthy, deeper, more meaningful relationships

The 7 Levels of Awareness

Human Awareness	Spiritual Awareness
Knowing Truth	God/Oneness
Sensing Truth	Mystics/Teachers
Speaking Truth	Spirit Guides
Emotional Feeling	Guardian Angels
Gut Feeling	Ancestors
Curiosity	Astral
Needs	Physical

We all start with our human needs when entering a physical body. Once our basic needs are met, then there is curiosity followed by feelings (gut and emotional), then truth emerges, speaking, sensing, and finally knowing truth. As we evolve on the human level, we are also moving up simultaneously on the spiritual side, becoming able to feel and receive spiritual guidance and higher levels of consciousness.

Knowing where you are on your journey helps you understand yourself and those around you. Being aware of where you are also helps you to have more compassion towards yourself as you continue on your path of personal growth and transformation.

Seeking Inner Wisdom

Release Your Goals

As you begin your journey toward higher consciousness and joy, you need to manage your mind and thoughts. Until you have control over your thoughts, it's essential to consciously occupy your mind with thoughts that will advance your life. When you dream big and set goals, you are future-pacing your life and giving your mind something positive to focus on, rather than allowing it to dwell on the past.

As you continue on the path to experiencing and expressing more joy in your life, you grow in consciousness. You begin to realize that there is a universal intelligence that knows more than you, knows what's best for you, and knows exactly what is needed to bring you more peace, happiness, and joy.

To allow universal intelligence to work its magic in your life, you must detach from your goals. This does not mean that you have no desires. It simply means that you set intentions, which help keep your mind focused, but you remain open to the

Universe delivering something better. When setting your intentions, ensure that when stating what you want, you add "**this or something better**." Remain open to magic showing up in your life.

"Ask for 'this' or something better."

When you set goals, you are expected to take steps toward achieving them. There are two ways of doing life: grace and process. Taking the steps to reach a goal requires a process, a plan of action.

When you set intentions, you are saying to the Universe, I would like to have this, but only if it's for my highest good, and if not, bring me something better. This, my friend, is called allowing grace.

You can only experience grace when you let go of control. Let go and trust the process of life itself. It's easier to let go when you have something else to cling to – so **let's exchange our goals for guidance**. Let's focus on developing our intuition.

What Is Intuition

From my book, "LadyUp: A Woman's Guide to Self-Defined Grace and Fearless Love."

Intuition is the ability to acquire knowledge without the use of reason. It's like a sixth sense. Everyone has it, but few choose to use it. It's like the elephant in the room that everyone chooses to ignore. Thought of as "too woo-woo" because it's not as tangible as the other five senses (sight, sound, smell, taste, and touch).

Only those who delve into the psychic realms are expected to explore and develop this sixth sense. The average person is expected to deny or ignore this amazing phenomenon that is a living, breathing part of who we are. Yet many successful businesspeople attribute their success to following their intuition. Many artists and musicians rely upon intuition as a guide for creative expression.

How Does Intuition Work?

The word 'intuition' comes from the Latin intueri, often translated as "to look inside" or "to contemplate."

Scientifically Speaking: Scientists say our subconscious mind absorbs every tiny detail we encounter, as well as every one of our experiences. It sees, records, and stores every subtle unit of information that the conscious mind does not pick up. Therefore, when making decisions, relying solely on the conscious mind for answers means we miss valuable information gathered and stored in the subconscious.

Just as the heart knows how to beat, when to beat, and how many times per minute to beat to keep us alive, so does the subconscious mind know precisely how to gather, record, and store important information that is vital to our health, safety, and well-being. It's a built-in survival mechanism that extends beyond our individual safety. It is designed to protect humanity and advance the species.

The subconscious mind communicates and guides us through feelings and impressions. During the dream state, while the conscious mind is resting, the subconscious is most active. This is one reason it's important to pay attention to our dreams. Albert Einstein received the theory of relativity in a dream. I think he was paying attention!

Spiritually Speaking: Spirituality teaches us that God speaks to us and guides us through our intuition. So, when we pray for answers and have faith, answers come through intuition —the ability to know without reason.

Whether there is a supernatural deity responding to our prayers, or the subconscious mind simply doing its job, just like the beating heart, I think we can all agree that there is something that looks over us. It guides us, tries to keep us safe, and helps us become more successful if we would but listen and trust. And, whatever it is that's providing such guidance, it's truly beyond the comprehension of our conscious reasoning mind. I refer to this as "Universal Intelligence."

When we tap into Universal Intelligence, we usually do the right thing, and not only do we win, but those around us also benefit. Imagine if we could get the entire world doing the right thing!

The first step is to reestablish and strengthen our connection to that universal intelligence, some call God or Spirit. Then we must be willing to listen, learn to trust it, and follow its guidance. The link that makes the connection possible is our feelings. Not our thoughts, not the thinking mind, not our intellect or logic, but our gut feelings.

The umbilical cord to Spirit is never severed. We are always nurtured through this feeling deep down in our guts, our instincts, and our knowingness.

We always pay a price when we ignore our gut feelings. However, because we live in a world where logic often takes precedence over instinct, we have learned to disregard our gut feelings and follow our heads. BIG MISTAKE!

It's typically easier for men to follow logic because they are wired to be linear thinkers, focused on the hunt. Women are not; women are the multitaskers and gatherers with diffused awareness, wired for expansion in all directions. This includes having greater access to feelings.

By combining intuition and reason, intuitive people appear to have a life advantage. Edith Jurka, M.D., says, "Intuitive persons have a sense of more ultimate control and advantages in life because intuition and right-brain functioning add creativity, humor, and the ability to solve problems, to reach goals, and to manage people more effectively."

Now, aren't you glad you're among the smarter folks by learning to lean into and trust your intuition? It's not only a good thing, but it's a powerful way of living.

Tapping Into Your Intuition

Tapping into your intuition involves quieting the mind and being open to the subtle signals our subconscious sends. Here are some ways to access it:

1. **Trust Your Gut**: Pay attention to those feelings and instincts that arise in moments of decision. Often, these are based on your subconscious mind's sifting through past experiences.

2. **Practice Mindfulness**: Meditation and mindfulness help to clear mental clutter, allowing you to become more attuned to your inner voice. The quieter the mind, the louder your intuition can become.

3. **Embrace Creativity**: Activities like journaling, painting, or free writing can stimulate intuitive thinking by allowing your mind to explore without limitations.

4. **Connect with Nature**: Spending time outdoors can also enhance intuition. The stillness and simplicity of nature help you reconnect with your deeper self, making it easier to access intuitive insights.

5. **Listen to Your Body**: Do you ever get goose bumps when truth hits you? Physical sensations often accompany intuitive thoughts. Pay attention to how your body reacts to situations—tightness in the chest or a sense of calm might signal what's right or wrong for you.

Incorporating these practices into your daily life can enhance your intuitive abilities, helping you make more informed and confident decisions.

Learning to Trust

It can be challenging to start listening to your intuition if you haven't practiced meditation. However, the benefits can be extremely rewarding and make life much easier. Once you have relaxed your body, focus your mind on a single thought or idea as you ask for guidance. Then sit in silence for as long as it feels right —10 or 15 minutes, or longer —and allow the guidance (ideas, insights) to flow freely. If unrelated images or messages appear, greet them with gratitude and let them pass. Please do not get caught up in them; let them move along, making way for new thoughts to enter. If you receive no thoughts or messages that are meaningful to your situation by the time you feel compelled to end your session, know that you WILL receive answers in divine timing. Trust this, and the answers may come to you during your day. They often come when you least expect them!

Learning to trust your intuition is simply acknowledging when you are right. Often, we say to ourselves, "Something told me to…" This is the voice of intuition. Even if you didn't follow it, acknowledge that it was there and give thanks for the awareness. Something was trying to offer guidance—be grateful.

At other times, you know something to be true, but you doubt. Learning to trust often means being still and observing before you jump in. Allow whatever is happening to simply unfold. Then you will know you were onto something. When we jump in and speak too soon, we often find we're off the mark. Intellect interferes. Be patient, allow whatever is happening to reveal itself, and you will find that you were right.

Beware of the ego. So often when we start hitting the target consistently, we get a big head and start thinking we always know what's right. Nothing shuts down the connection faster than ego taking over. Be humble in that which you come to know and handle your wisdom with responsibility.

Start listening to and trusting your intuition; it will guide you to places you never dreamed possible. This is a step toward leading the surrendered life as the Servant.

LEVEL 4 - THE SERVANT (Fully Awake)

Level 4 ~ Giving What *Is* Needed

The **"Servant"** walks the path of surrender and leads a joy-filled Life. The level of consciousness is **Fully Awake.**

Benefits of Being Fully Awake

- You are motivated by inspiration
- Inspiration dictates intention
- Intention leads to inspired actions
- Inspired actions led to embracing your calling with grace and ease *(there is no efforting)*
- Your life becomes joyful and magical!

Thy Will Be Done

She Let Go ...

Without a thought or a word, she let go.

She let go of fear.

She let go of judgments.

She let go of the confluence of opinions swarming around her head.

She let go of the committee of indecision within her.

She let go of all the 'right' reasons.

Wholly and completely, without hesitation or worry,

She just let go.

She didn't ask anyone for advice.

She didn't read a book on how to let go

She just let go.

She let go of all the memories that held her back.

She let go of all of the anxiety that kept her from moving forward.

She let go of the planning and all of the calculations about how to do it just right.

She didn't promise to let go.

She didn't journal about it.

She didn't write the projected date in her Day-Timer.

She made no public announcement.

She didn't check the weather report or read her daily horoscope.

She just let go.

She didn't analyze whether she should let go.

She didn't call her friends to discuss the matter.

She didn't utter one word.

She just let go.

No one was around when it happened. There was no applause or congratulations.

No one thanked her or praised her. No one noticed a thing.

Like a leaf falling from a tree,

She just let go.

There was no effort. There was no struggle.

It wasn't good. It wasn't bad.

It was what it was, and it is just that.

In the space of letting go, she let it all be.

A small smile came over her face.

A light breeze blew through her

And the sun and the moon shone forevermore.

Here's to giving ourselves the gift of letting go...

There's only one guru ~ YOU

(The author of this poem is unclear. A few sites list Ernest Holmes as the author, another Jennifer Eckert Bernau, and still another Rev. Safire Rose.)

What if we all pretended it was easy?

A Statement of Grace

Someone asked, "What is GRACE?"

Grace carries you and takes you beyond the struggle, beyond the pain. Grace is expansive and is not bound by time and space. With Grace, all things are possible. Grace is an energy that surrounds us individually and collectively; it is with us always. We must first learn to acknowledge, then trust, then know, and surrender to it. Whatever you're fighting, whatever your struggles, call forth grace. Whatever your needs, your dreams, your goals, call forth grace. Whenever your heart aches, your body aches, call forth grace.

GRACE is a universal energy that serves humanity at its core. Call upon it, then surrender to it all of you.

The Road to Surrender

Life Mastery takes you on the road to surrender. When you have found peace and happiness, and your Soul is calling you deeper, it's time to surrender. It's time to move beyond personal ambition and embrace your calling. This is the road to surrender.

On the road to surrender, there will be times when you will become stuck in traffic. You won't know which way to go or what to do. This is the time to trust your intuition.

Years ago, my first husband and I were vacationing in Hawaii. We rented a car to explore the Big Island. Darkness arrived before we knew it, and we were still out and about, having a great time. Soon, we found ourselves in pitch blackness on a lonely road, not sure where we were headed. In those days, you had a Thomas Guide or a printed map for navigation. As we were driving along, I suddenly yelled STOP! He slammed on the brakes. We didn't know why until we got out of the car and the headlights revealed a cliff just a few feet ahead. There were no road barriers to warn us, only my keen intuition and guidance. You all have this, but often don't listen.

Intellect says one thing, and wisdom says another. It's a long journey from the head to the heart. To make the trip not only more tolerable but more enjoyable, you are invited to rise above it all and capture a different perspective. Aren't there times when you wish you were a bird with a bird's eye view? What about the times you're stuck in traffic and wish you had a helicopter to fly above it all? Whenever you feel stuck in life, you can truly rise above it.

You Can Learn to Fly!

1. Find a safe and comfortable place inside to lie down, not outside. You need walls to set the limits for this exercise. Don't lie in your bed because you don't want to fall asleep. Lie on your back and gently close your eyes. If you have the means, a cover over your eyes would be a nice addition. Perhaps a pillow to cradle your head and support your neck. Maybe even a light throw to cover your body.

2. Imagine yourself lifting out of your body and rising high, high, higher. You can see the ceiling with your eyes closed. You can easily and effortlessly rise high enough to meet the ceiling. You will automatically stop rising when you reach your personal limits. You won't go too far; the ceiling is there to keep yourself contained within your space.

3. From this high advantage point, look down at your body lying comfortably and safely. What is in the room surrounding your body? What are the objects, the colors? Stay here as long as it feels good, then gently allow yourself to float back down —down, down, down —slowly merging back into your body. Begin wiggling your toes and fingers. Stretch your body. Notice how good it feels now to be back connected. Also, notice what it felt like to be outside of your body as the observer.

Practice being the observer every day until you feel comfortable enough to go beyond the walls of your room. Take a trip outside and see what's around your house. Caution: Don't travel inside or through anyone else's house or private space. You don't need to pick up anyone's negative energy on your travels. Just float and feel the lightness of being. This is you without a body, without attachments. This is YOU!

This exercise does not permit you to escape this third-dimensional reality; it merely shows you that you are not a body, that you are so much more than a body. It shows you that the things you're attached to are attached to the body and not you. They have no real meaning or significance in the grander sense of life. The higher you rise, the smaller things appear.

From this point of view, you can see how small you've been playing. You can see how small your problems are. You can see your past and all of your so-called mistakes. You can see all the bumps and bruises others have put you through. You can see the road behind you.

From this vantage point, you can also, if you will, see your future. You can see the road you want to take. You can see what experiences you'd like to have. You can see the value of having a body to go through these experiences. You can see that you are in charge of your life and your body.

Whenever you feel stuck, rise above, look at the road behind you, and all that you've come through. Look ahead and decide which path you'd like to take going forward. Then settle back into your body, your vehicle, and get moving in that direction.

Now you might say, the path is not clear. Use your imagination and let it take you to a special place. A place in time that you truly long for, a place where you will find peace, love, health, and happiness.

What are you looking for on your road to surrender? Are you seeking better health? How would your life look different? Are you seeking more money? How would your life look different? Are you seeking more loving relationships? How would your life look different if you had what you want? Imagine having it – that's the path you take. Go in that direction, and the universe will support you and show you the way. Trust your intuition.

When you feel stuck, you seek clarity. But sometimes, **clarity can get in the way of progress.** Sometimes you must follow your intuition and trust the unknown. Let go of needing to know everything in advance. Living the surrendered life means you only get to know what is necessary for you to take the next step, and nothing more. When you know too much, you try to control the situation, and you end up getting in the way. Less is sometimes better. Let go and let God.

Living in the "Let Go"
The Surrendered Life

There is a part of you that loves to reminisce over the past, whether it's old songs, lovers, places you've lived and/or worked, or certain aromas to awaken the senses. You don't stop at the "good old days." You also venture into the darker side of your younger days, the days when pain was your closest friend, and no one could comfort you in a way that made a difference. You reminisce over the pain of the past, even though it may be long gone. It's still a part of your tapestry, a part of you.

You can choose to forget certain aspects of your past, but you can never truly release them; to do so would be to take away some of the very fabric of your being. We want to acknowledge all of who we are and honor those seemingly broken parts of ourselves that have learned to survive over the years. It's the survival mechanisms that we want to transform, not necessarily release. We ARE whole, perfect, and complete just as we are. However, we know that we can live a happier, healthier life by realizing more of our potential. We can only do this by releasing the past safety mechanisms that we have held in place for so long.

When there is resistance to releasing the past, other factors are typically at play, such as unprocessed anger or a desire for revenge. In any event, you must be aware that your feelings of anger or thoughts of revenge only strengthen the pattern that has been put in place to keep you safe. The stronghold that it has on you will keep you stuck in the past, with the hopes that someday, you will be made whole. Not realizing that you are already whole, you just need to allow yourself to see it, accept it, and be it.

The best reason to let go of things is to free your mind, body, and soul for greater, more fulfilling experiences in life. If you want to live a prosperous life, you'll want to let go of those things that hold you back and take you down.

There are three areas of life where letting go is necessary. **Mental anguish, emotional baggage**, and unnecessary **physical/material possessions**. All three require the same process, just a different focus. Remember, your focus is what directs the flow of energy within and around you. That energy within you guides and directs your life experiences. Shift the focus and direction of energy, and you shift the quality of your life.

Mental anguish is primarily due to emotional baggage. Emotional baggage often results from past programming. You have been programmed for protection. When you can disrupt the programming and install a new, updated program, your life will change. To update your programming, look at the stories you're telling yourself about where you are and what's going on.

Two major causes of pain are attachments and expectations. You can be attached to a toxic person or to a place with a toxic vibe. You can become attached to things like TV dramas, food, drugs, or bad habits.

You came into this world with nothing, and you will leave this world with nothing. During your visit here, you have become attached to things that evoke certain emotions. These attachments are what cause pain and suffering. Because you have these attachments in your life, you have come to expect certain things to appear in specific ways. These expectations can lead to disappointment when not met.

What you are letting go of is not the person, place, or thing that's causing the problem; you are letting go of your expectations and attachment to the person, place, or thing you've come to know.

The Letting Go Process

1. **Honesty** - Finish this sentence: **"Right now, the biggest or hardest thing for me to release and let go of is (name the person, place, or thing)."**

2. **Truth** – acknowledge where you are and take full responsibility for being there, in that place, that situation, whether you consciously signed up for it or not. Declare for yourself: **"I realize this is an attachment, and I am willing to let go of the attachment right now."**

3. **Choice** – take back your power. Realize that you are not a victim of circumstance. You have the power to either change what is or change your perception of what is to create a better experience for your life. Repeat this statement: **"I ask for the guidance to change the situation, or that my eyes be opened to see things differently, and my heart be filled with compassion.**

4. **Actions** – It is said that actions speak louder than words. The way you live your life and show up in the world determines how people will treat you. Repeat: **"From this day forward, I easily and gracefully let go of anything and anyone that is not in alignment with my highest good. I take full responsibility for my choices in life, and I always stand in my truth."**

In Summary:

1. "Right now, the biggest or hardest thing for me to release and let go of is (name the person, place, or thing)."

2. "I realize this is an attachment, and I am willing to let go of the attachment right now."

3. "I ask for the guidance to change the situation, or that my eyes be opened to see things differently, and my heart be filled with compassion."

4. "From this day forward, I easily and gracefully let go of anything and anyone that is not in alignment with my highest good. I take full responsibility for my choices in life, and I always stand in my truth."

Remember, you have already awakened from the Dreamer state of consciousness by practicing eternal forgiveness and releasing past emotional baggage. Forgive yourself, forgive everyone in your world, and forgive every unpleasant situation.

A Universal Prayer:

Unconditional love and eternal forgiveness, I extend to everyone and every situation: amazing mercy and clear guidance I receive with grace and ease. Filled with inner peace, I rest in Thee. Thy will be done.

That first step —honesty —is often the hardest to take. Usually, you don't want to know the truth, so it's just easier to live in denial. You may be afraid of what the truth will reveal, or fearful of the actions the truth will require that you take.

Be honest with yourself first. Then it is your responsibility to be honest with others. Once you have the courage to know, it will become easier to do what you must do – let go.

Exercise for Surrender

Think about what has held you back in the past. It may have been feeling like you didn't have enough of something. Not enough money, not enough time, not enough space, not enough education, not enough exposure or recognition, not enough support, etc. Just think about whatever it was that you felt held you back, or is holding you back. Now, visualize a basket of different-colored balloons before you. (In the future, you can use a basket of real balloons if you want to add substance to this process.) Think about the thing that you feel has held you back. Allow whatever emotion that brings up for you to surface. It may make you feel small, like you are not enough. It may make you feel scared. It may make you want to run and hide. It may make you want to scream. Just allow whatever feelings you experience to come up for you when you think about what has held you back.

Now, in your mind's eye, choose a balloon from your imaginary basket of balloons. And, as you allow yourself to feel that emotion, blow all of it into the balloon. Taking several deep breaths and releasing that energy into the balloon will help you fully release every emotion associated with the situation. You have a basket full of balloons in front of you, so feel free to use as many as you need. Just get it all out.

Now see yourself tying off the balloons, one at a time, and then releasing them. See them taking off, rising higher and higher as you say to yourself, "I surrender and I let go of any and all limited thinking, and I now create the space within me for something better.

Prayer of Surrender

Once you've released the last balloon, take a moment to center yourself with a few deep breaths. In this moment, imagine what it would feel like to be totally surrounded by God's love. Think about what is troubling you. Now, pray this prayer of surrender:

Dear God,

I am open to your perfect love, moving me beyond the appearances I see. I know that divine right action is taking place at this very moment, and I trust that your will is being done right here and right now. I pray for peace of mind and divine guidance for all concerned, including myself, knowing that you are fully in charge. I surrender my judgments. I surrender my ego. I surrender my need to be in control. I simply get out of the way, and I let go. Amen.

Total Surrender

Total surrender truly is walking in blind faith. It's not knowing the future and being comfortable in not knowing. When you are not comfortable, you tend to want to give up, and there's an energy of sadness and hopelessness. This is not surrender. Surrender is a conscious decision to rise above the situation. It's turning the problem over to a higher power. To surrender is to completely sever your attachment to the outcome and know that all is well.

When you set your intention towards a specific outcome and then let go, stating, "this or something better," you have given the situation direction and a command. The Universe will carry it out from there. If you don't give the situation a direction, you are giving up and hoping for the best.

You can, indeed, reap the best from giving up; however, you are leaving much to chance. The Universe will always respond in like energy. If the quality of your energy is one of letting go of struggle, you will find yourself at ease, even if you may not achieve the best outcome. If the quality of the energy you are letting go of was directed toward a specific outcome, you will find there is grace in the unfolding of the situation. You may also be pleasantly surprised by the outcome!

Whatever you're holding on to has a hold on you.

We must learn to walk with an open hand, holding on to nothing.

PART IV – BEYOND THE CALLING

BEYOND MY CALLING

We've talked a lot about "purpose," your reason for being. Your Calling goes deeper than your purpose. Your purpose can change as you grow older and more mature. Your purpose today may be to teach children. Once you retire, you may find that your purpose shifts, drawing you to travel the world and explore different cultures and how people live in other parts of the globe.

Purpose refers to the overarching reason for our existence or the core motivation behind what we do. It's often a broad and timeless concept that drives us to seek meaning in life. Our purpose may center on values such as love, growth, helping others, or seeking happiness. It's the "why" behind our actions—why we get out of bed each day, why we pursue certain goals, or why we make certain choices. It's deeply personal and often evolves as we grow and change.

Calling, on the other hand, is more specific. It refers to a particular path or role we feel destined to fulfill. A calling is often seen as a unique, deeply fulfilling task or mission that aligns with our talents and passions. It's something we feel drawn to, something that resonates with us on a soul level. A calling might be a career, an artistic pursuit, or a life of service. It's typically something that feels larger than just personal ambition and is tied to making a meaningful impact in the world.

In short, **purpose** is the broad, internal motivation for life, while **calling** is the more specific path or action that reflects that purpose. Your calling is how you express your purpose in the world. Your calling is what brings you pure joy and soul satisfaction.

Embracing your calling is a deeply personal journey that requires self-awareness, courage, and commitment. It involves aligning your actions with your passions and strengths while staying true to what resonates deeply within you.

Embracing Your Calling

Listen to Your Inner Voice: Pay attention to moments when you feel most alive, fulfilled, or at peace. These moments often point to your true calling. Trust your intuition and reflect on activities or causes that light you up. What are you naturally drawn to, even when challenges arise?

Identify Your Strengths and Passions: Your calling often lies at the intersection of your talents and your passions. What are you good at, and what do you love doing? Identifying these qualities can provide you with valuable insight into your path. Remember that your calling may not always be something obvious, but it's something that feels meaningful and authentic to you.

Step Out of Your Comfort Zone: Embracing your calling often means taking risks and stepping into the unknown. It requires letting go of old habits or fears that hold you back. Courage is essential, as it is trust that taking steps toward your calling will lead you to growth, even if the path is uncertain.

Take Action: Don't wait for the "perfect moment" or for everything to fall into place. Start small by taking concrete steps toward your calling. Whether it's pursuing a hobby, making a career change, or volunteering, each action brings you closer to living your purpose.

Persist Through Challenges: The road to fulfilling your calling isn't always easy. Obstacles will arise, and doubts may creep in. However, perseverance is key. Stay committed, knowing that obstacles often teach valuable lessons that shape your journey.

Seek Support and mentorship: Surround yourself with people who support and encourage your journey. Find mentors, coaches, or like-minded individuals who can offer guidance and insight as you walk the path toward embracing your calling.

Trust the Process: Embracing your calling isn't always linear, and the timing may not be immediate. Trust that the steps you take, even if they seem small, are leading you in the right direction. Be patient with yourself and recognize that your calling may unfold over time.

By cultivating self-awareness, trusting your inner guidance, and actively pursuing your passion, you can embrace your calling with confidence and purpose. It's about aligning your everyday life with what feels true to your heart, allowing you to make a meaningful impact on the world around you.

To become motivated and inspired, you need to know what your Soul wants for you. Go back to the chapter on "Purpose" and review your answers to those very important questions, including:

1. What activities bring me the most joy?
2. What values are important to me?
3. What am I most passionate about?
4. What would others say is my claim to fame?
5. What positive impact would I like to have on the world?

A Prayer to Pray Daily

I open my mind and my heart to the perfect flow of Universal Intelligence to use my gifts and talents for extraordinary good in the world. I surrender my ego and embrace my Soul's desires.

What *is* Beyond Your Calling

What lies beyond your calling is a connection so deep with Spirit that you swim in an ocean of oneness. The lines of separation and duality cease to exist. There is no longer external power; you are the first cause of all that occurs in your world. You become the light that you had been waiting for. You have a keen understanding of your mission - to simply be the light. With each breath you take in, you realize it's no longer an automatic process of releasing and letting go of the breath; it's a conscious choice to remain as you are, or to transmute all that has been identified as you.

It is not only the vibration of the master teacher that walks this path; it is truly the mystic. It takes courage to stand at this level of majesty to witness the totality of all that is. It takes a desire to transcend your individual calling and own the world, where there is no longer a calling, simply effortless being.

Going beyond your calling is having the courage to be fully present in each moment and surrender moment-by-moment to the desires echoing from the depths of your Soul.

When you're ready to go beyond, ready for the total expansion of the Soul, take a deep, deep, deep breath in, close your eyes, and exhale with full force —really blow it out, emptying the belly. Now rest in the pause with your eyes closed for as long as it's comfortable. Do not fight or struggle; just be still and inhale when it's time. As you practice this exercise, you will find that you remain longer and longer in the sacred pause of life. It is within this space that consciousness expands, and internal power is generated as you connect with all that is, in absolute oneness.

When you are able to tap into the vastness of who you are as a spiritual being, your physical body will not be able to contain the intensity of love, and tears of joy and ecstasy will flow. It is at this point that most people will feel they have found complete soul satisfaction. They will know what it feels like to go beyond their calling and into oneness. The key, then, is to practice being in that sacred space and vibration as you walk through your daily life.

Life mastery is not a destiny; it's a journey. As you continue to walk the spiritual path, radiating your inner light, people will be drawn to you for various reasons. You remain human and must abide by this world of duality. It is the wise person who protects their energy and does not allow others to drain it. Be unapologetically selfish with who you spend your time with and whom you serve. Be guided by the light within, and you will always be blessed beyond your wildest dreams.

Accept that magic happens for you, through you, and as you all the time. This is your new way of being in the world, your new norm.

VOICE OF THE MASTER

Master Your Life!

Life Mastery is about having a clear vision and learning to manage your mental and emotional state.

Clear Vision: This comes from knowing what you want, what makes you happy, and brings you joy.

Managing Your Mind (Attitude): This is achieved through Positive Affirmations. Declare your truth. Meditate for guidance and calmness.

Managing your Emotional State (Gratitude): This is done by living in a state of gratitude for all that is, all that has been, and all that is to come.

From Pain to Power

Spirit Speaks on Pain to Power
(Channeled session with Wanda Marie)

Living the surrendered life requires approaching the idea with a beginner's mind. You've learned so much of what is wrong, and your mind has been cluttered with fear. You are afraid of failure, afraid of success, afraid of what others may think, do, or say. Afraid of living, afraid of dying. The truth is, there is absolutely nothing to fear at all. It is said that humans truly fear only two things: falling and loud noises. These are both attached to survival of the body. You are not your body. You are Spirit in the flesh. You have been confused for so long, thinking you were a body. Once you let go of the notion that you are a body and begin to realize your divinity as Spirit, you will be free. Not only will you be free mentally, but you will know what it means to take control of your body and turn your pain to power.

There is mental pain, emotional pain, and physical pain. They are all the same. Pain causes different degrees of discomfort, but all pain stems from the root chakra, the center of survival.

> *Pain stems from the root chakra,*
> *the center of survival.*

Let's not distinguish between the different areas of pain or the different degrees of discomfort. Let us focus on the fact that pain causes focused energy. Because it is designed to get your attention, it requires your focus. If you try to deny pain the attention it deserves, it worsens and can become excruciating. It can get to the point of taking away your very breath and taking away your very life.

There is nothing so dominating to the human experience as pain. You have free will. You can allow the pain to consume you and take you out, or you can rise up and allow it to empower you. Thus, pain to power.

When you decide to rise above, you will look at pain in a whole new light. You will see that it was and is your teacher. You will know that it was or is demanding something from you. Once you become aware of what pain is asking of you, you can work together to heal your mind of ill thoughts, which in turn affects your emotions and how you feel. How you feel filters down to the body, influencing physical expressions such as healing.

Your physical body is meant to transmit energy focused for a purpose. When you are not on purpose, your body will let you know. Your mind will know first, as you will see the red flags. Just because the red flags are there does not mean you are paying attention to them. You have a choice. You can listen and adjust, or ignore the signs and keep moving in the same direction.

The second level of awareness comes through your gut. You will feel that something is off when you are out of alignment. You will not feel good, happy, healthy, or alive. Your body is the final sign that you are out of alignment with your purpose. Pain is your spiritual GPS.

Pain is designed to awaken you to your true potential. It is your spiritual GPS

QUESTION: *Why am I in pain even though I know I'm following my passion and living in alignment with my purpose?*

Pain is restricted energy. Even though you may think you are on purpose, somewhere along the line, you have stifled the energy. You may have gotten comfortable or felt you could not do more or go further. You may be tired and ready to quit. Pain is there to awaken you to more of your potential, reminding you that you were built for more; keep going.

QUESTION: *But what if I am tired?*

Then you have taken on too much control; letting go is about releasing control. If you know how to reach your goal, it is not big enough for God. Your goals should be beyond your reach and therefore beyond your control. When you are aligned with your purpose, there is a natural flow of energy within you, moving through you and guiding you. There is little for you to do. It is considered effortless being. You will be amazed at how much you get done by doing very little when you're operating within the flow. When the ego gets in the way and starts controlling the process, the energy gets depleted, and the Soul becomes weary. It's like being in the kitchen preparing to bake a cake, and you've got it all together. Then someone walks in and takes over. You would become weary and exhausted, finding yourself in a power struggle with the other person. You do not want to be in a power struggle with your ego, so let go and let God be in charge. Go with the flow, and you will not be tired; you will be inspired and empowered.

Dealing With Loss

QUESTION: *What about the pain of loss? What is that trying to teach me, and how do I manage it?*

You may not believe this, but there is no such thing as loss. The concept of loss refers to the human condition of survival. Attachments cause pain and suffering. This is why some people are taught to walk with an open hand, holding on to nothing.

The lesson is to know the truth. You are not your body; therefore, as Spirit, you cannot be physically attached to anything in the material world. You believe that you are connected to someone, another body, and when that body no longer exists on the same plane with you, you feel a void.

Return to your spiritual essence, and you will see that no connection has been lost due to the body returning to dust. The Soul you knew still exists. As long as you identify as a body, you will feel loss and grief when another body transitions. It is customary to entertain such feelings of loss. Times are shifting, and the world is starting to understand truth. You are beginning to have celebrations of life when a Soul departs. This is a step in the right direction. You celebrate the body coming forth as a newborn baby, so shall you celebrate the departing of the Soul, knowing it has fulfilled its mission.

QUESTION: *But how do we know when a soul has fulfilled its mission?*

You will know when the Soul has fulfilled its mission by its departure. Some souls come and extend their stay after fulfilling their mission. These are the people you say are like cats —have nine lives. Then some are stillborn and never see the light of day.

Life Mastery

They have indeed fulfilled their mission as well, and their parents are moving through the lessons left within the Soul's wake.

QUESTION: *So how do I get rid of the pain?*

Pain has an energy all its own, designed to demand attention. The way to alleviate pain is to become aware of what it wants from you. To become aware, you must stop, listen, and follow directions.

1. **Stop:** Locate the pain point. Acknowledge it with forgiveness of self, others, and the situation. Stand in gratitude for the way the pain has served you. The pain may be in your head as a headache, in your heart as an attack, or somewhere in your body.

2. **Listen:** Get still and quiet so you can listen. Then focus on the point of pain and ask,

    - "What do you want from me?"
    - "What are you teaching me?"
    - "What are you protecting me from?"
    - "Do I still need this protection? If so, what is a better way for me to receive this protection?"

    Sit in stillness and observation for 10 to 15 minutes and listen. Yes, there will be crazy thoughts running through your head as the monkey mind persists. But the longer you sit still and allow those insignificant thoughts to just pass through, the clearer you become, and the truth can begin to surface.

3. **Follow Directions: The truth will surface, and it will startle you!** You will feel it in your soul when it's revealed. You may want to turn away from it, but you will know it

when it hits you. Be ready to receive the truth and follow your guidance. Pain will tell you what it needs from you. The truth will set you free.

You may not get clear during your first sitting; it really depends on how deep the pain goes. If you are in severe pain, it may be difficult to sit still and relax. But the more you attempt this practice of stillness and observation, regardless of the intensity of the pain, it will begin to lessen. Observe the thoughts running through your mind. They are not "your" thoughts; they are thoughts within mass consciousness that you have agreed to entertain. Let them go. Allow the thoughts to float about you, without getting attached. It is said in meditation that if you see the Buddha, slay him. This means that you do not even allow deities to distract you. Stay focused on discovering what the pain is trying to tell you. Breathe deep and relax—watch the thoughts float by. Again, the truth will startle you! You will not be able to miss it. When given the space, truth speaks loud and clear! Wait for it. You cannot rush it. Be still and know.

As you sit in stillness and observation, in reflection and communication, you may want to journal your insights. Journaling can help you stay focused and not get stuck. If a thought surfaces that deserves some attention, write it down and move on; don't linger. You can give that thought your attention later.

Releasing Physical Pain

1. **Drink water to flush out the system**. Plain water, not colored or flavored. Even if you don't like the taste of water, drink it anyway. If you are in a lot of physical pain, drink plenty of water. Water is the liquid essence of God. Drench your body with this energy and set your intention that as you receive the water into your body, you are

receiving the healing energy of God. Water is cleansing and purifying, consume this God energy freely. Take showers and allow the healing energy to wash over you.

2. **Fill the body with Light.** White Light, known as the Christ Light, carries the highest vibrational frequency of love for healing. Your root chakra, the center of survival, is located at your tailbone and is known as the color red. Use the power of your Imagination to bring the White Light from the cosmos, down through your crown, through your body, and into the tailbone area. See the White Light swirling around the red root chakra, turning the red to a light pink and then fading into the White Light. This process cleanses and purifies the root chakra, dissolves unnecessary fear of survival, and clears the path for healing on all levels. The Light is potent, let it in to transform your pain into power.

3. **Breathe deeply.** When you are in pain, you tend to breathe shallowly rather than inhaling and exhaling fully. Your breath is the breath of God. Receive it with intention and release it with intention. As you breathe in, speak your word for health and healing. "I inhale health and exhale love." At this point, you are not releasing pain. This is not the time to focus on pain; you do that during your time of stillness and observation. As you go about your day, notice your breathing patterns, and affirm that you are taking in healing energy and releasing more love into the world. Love is the ultimate healer – use it!

There is power within your pain. When you do the work, you can stop focusing on the pain, and you'll be able to use that energy and power to fuel your passion. Your passion leaves clues about your life's purpose. Being aware of and aligned with your purpose helps you overcome most of the pain you will encounter.

You are not your body, but you do have a body, and you will have pain from time to time to remind you to stop and pay attention. The more you stay focused on your purpose, the quicker you will be able to eliminate pain when it hits.

When you have a greater purpose than your pain, you will be able to move a little further down the road to surrender. When you have no passion, no drive, and no direction, pain becomes your closest companion, and the relationship grows until you turn your attention to something more meaningful, something that makes you more excited about life. What are you living for? Are you living for pain relief? Are you waiting for the pain to end before you begin to live? If so, shift your mindset. Decide right now that you have a greater purpose than the pain. Decide right now that you are ready to be more, have more, and do more to live an amazing life.

QUESTION: *Why do I need a plan if I'm just going to surrender?*

The pain is or was your wakeup call. You are awake now. You have done your stillness and observation exercise, reflected, and communicated with the pain, so you know what you need to do. Create your plan of action. Remember, man plans, and God laughs. So, make sure your plan is too big for you to accomplish without God. Make sure that your plan is merely an idea of the direction you would like to take, but remain open to Spirit's guidance. This is the road to surrender.

Having a plan keeps you focused on something other than pain. Remember, an idle mind is the devil's playground. Stay focused and on purpose with a plan of action. And stay open and surrender to Spirit leading the way.

It takes courage to surrender, especially if you think you know the right direction for your life. The road to surrender means you are a passenger, not the driver. It means there may be roadblocks, detours, forks in the road, flat tires, and more, but you never worry, because you're just along for the ride—God's in the driver's seat.

Focus your attention and energy on your purpose. It is said that the pain pushes until the vision pulls. What are you envisioning for yourself, for your life? Use the pain as fuel to get you going and power you up! Energy follows focus and determines your experiences.

Purpose is often disguised as something other than what you imagined. To find your true purpose, you must rise above survival. You know you are on purpose when you are happy doing whatever you are doing. Happy, not just content, truly happy. When you are truly happy with your life, you can't wait to get out of bed each day and get going!

Comfort Zones Are Danger Zones

QUESTION: *What's the difference between being at peace and being content or happy?*

One can be at peace and be happy. No one can be content and truly happy. Content energy settles for what is rather than striving for what could be. Many people claim to be happy and content. What they are really saying is, "I'm comfortable and don't want to move out of my comfort zone. It's safe here, so I'm happy."

Comfort zones are danger zones. If you are not growing, you are dying.

QUESTION: *Why can't I grow within my comfort zone?*

You can, but only by expanding your comfort zone. You push the limits a bit, learn something new, master it, and then become comfortable again. The trouble is that some forget to keep expanding, especially as the body ages and weakens. Learning something new requires more energy and mental effort. Growing old comes quicker the more settled you are in your comfort zone. As you continue to grow and expand your consciousness, you will be healthier and happier during your life's journey.

QUESTION: *So really, how do I turn this pain into power?*

Remember, pain stems from the root chakra, the center of survival. Survival is the strongest human instinct. Survival energy is powerful! The fight to survive is that live-or-die energy within you. That instinct, your root chakra, is your seat of power and can propel you into the future, beyond the present moment, beyond the body sensations, beyond pain. The future is where you fulfill your purpose. Once your purpose has been fulfilled, you have a choice to stay a little longer and play or move on into the next dimension of so-called space and time.

So many people commit suicide, consciously and subconsciously, because they have lost their way and have nothing to live for. They are so confused about life; they would rather end it and start over. When the pain becomes that severe, it's time to seek help. Before it gets that dire, do a little soul searching to find out:

1. Why are you here on this planet? Your purpose, your mission.

2. What you need to do to get on the right path and in alignment with what you came to do.

3. If you are content, find out what you need to do to grow to the next level. Don't get suck into the danger zone, keep moving!

There is power within your pain. Stop focusing on the pain and explore the power it provides. Discover your purpose ~ Your passion leaves clues!

Deep Surrender

Spirit Speaks on Surrender
(Channeled session with Wanda Marie)

QUESTION: *I am tired, and I do want to surrender the struggle. How can I shift this energy?*

By providing direction for your thought process, you will naturally shift the energy to a more positive nature. When you dwell on being tired, you will only create more struggle. When you focus your energy on the outcome you wish to see unfold, your entire vibration will be lifted, and your energy will shift. The key is maintaining that shift. Once you know what you'd like to see differently, go back to the basic principles of VAM (visualization, affirmation, and meditation). Visualize what you want to see differently, speak your word (name it, claim it, own it), be still, ask for guidance (what is mine to do, what is my next step?). Then listen and be inspired.

QUESTION: *I'm told to keep praying for something until I get it. What are your thoughts on this?*

When you pray (ask), listen to your guidance, and obey, that's often walking in blind faith. When you can trust the Universe to that degree, you have arrived at deep surrender. You have engaged your mind with the outcome, then let go of it all at once.

The ultimate prayer is seeking oneness with God. When you are praying, asking the Universe for something, you are engaging in the concept of separation. This is the greatest disease of mankind. The illusion of separation has everyone thinking there is something outside of themselves to get. There is only something to "be." You already possess all that you could desire. You must only realize your oneness with God.

The idea of praying or continually asking for something is begging. The more you beg, the further you push that which you desire away from you. Because the more you beg, the more you feel the "need" for it.

QUESTION: *Wait, what? What does all that mean?*

When you pray from a place of knowing you already have that which you seek, you are merely requesting a vibrational shift in energy so that you may be in alignment with your desires. Everything is energy, vibration, and frequency. If you are experiencing lack, the sensation is there to reveal to you a lack of energy vibrating at the frequency you need for your desires to be made manifest in the dimension you are occupying at this time.

It simply means you get to experience that which you are energetically aligned with. And, because you were born with free will, you get to decide what you should align with. There's no such thing as good or bad; there is only energy, and you get to declare the quality of that energy and what it means for you. How you decide to affirm or validate the energy determines the experiences you draw into your world, your life.

When you set goals, it is, in essence, a prayer or request for something outside of yourself. A goal is something you want to accomplish or achieve. In the achievement, there is a feeling of confidence, self-esteem, gratitude, and power. With deep surrender, you have gratitude. Because deep surrender requires grace, no actual effort on your part, you don't get that sense of true accomplishment. You must be willing to let go of the need to feel powerful in order to embrace the joy of gratitude.

Thoughts to Ponder

1. Soul is the Spirit's vehicle. The Soul evolves to become more and more aware of itself as Spirit.

2. Karma means action.

3. The process of creation is Love (grace) and Law (order).

4. We change our past consequences every time we see the actions differently.

5. Cooperation versus competition is the solution to the world's problems.

6. Heaven means expansion.

7. There are 3 purposes in the universe: (1) to love, (2) to be loved, and (3) to grow in the process.

8. A guru (teacher) awakens you to your own awareness. As you grow, you attract more advanced teachers.

9. There are 7 elements of God

    1. Light
    2. Love
    3. Power
    4. Peace
    5. Order
    6. Beauty
    7. Joy

10. When you bring energy into form, you experience its full potential, which is both good and bad, all opposites.

11. Ignorance simply means to ignore the truth.

12. To examine your deepest sorrow, you can find your greatest joy.

Life Mastery

13. Judgment is your own consciousness. God does not judge, and Christ does not condemn.

14. Grace is the omnipresence of God's unconditional love.

15. When behavior determines the depth of your love, it is conditional.

16. To listen well, repeat what is said silently to yourself.

17. Communion means to partake of the presence of God within.

18. Repent means to change.

19. If not well prepared, the rescuers can become the victims.

20. You are the sum total of all you have ever been.

21. Consider yourself with visions unlimited.

22. Death is first a conscious choice, then an unconscious process.

23. Disease is an accepted suicide by society.

24. You can educate yourselves on how to gracefully make your transition *(leave the physical body and enter into another dimension)*.

25. Transcendence is to take your body with you. It will adapt to its new environment through your consciousness.

26. People are not usually afraid of dying, but are afraid of the process, how it will occur.

27. What's true on one dimension is true on all.

28. Truth allows you to escape the karmic wheel.

29. Intuition is your link to the absolute, the "Inner Teacher."

30. The Mystic Realm is the absolute; it is truth, the source, where angels work to bring you closer to God. There is no fear, and it is changeless.

31. The psychic realm also includes the astral plane, where all types of spirits work for various purposes. This realm is of truth and error and is changeable. It involves some fear.

32. Intuition means "inner teacher." Get uncomplicated, go directly to the source within.

33. As you transcend in thought, the angels descend to meet you, and you work together on common ground.

34. One moment of success erases years of failure.

35. You are all light workers; you are the light of the physical world. You are preparing now for what you are yet to become.

36. Problems: Do not ignore them, acknowledge them, look at them, but do not embrace them. They exist as only experiences, but not truth.

7 Rules to Win at Life Mastery

1. Slow down, relax, and stay calm – regardless.
2. Prioritize and protect your joy – always.
3. Everyone is your teacher – be grateful.
4. Every event is just an event – be mindful.
5. Life is a mystery and a miracle - enjoy it.
6. You are a gift to the world - know it.
7. Give what you came to give – just do it!

Dear Life Mastery Student,

It's amazing how far you've come…

I'm writing to you from a future that once felt like a distant dream—one you only whispered about in quiet moments of longing. And yet, here you are. You've done it. You've awakened. You've risen. You've remembered who you truly are.

You've become a person who radiates certainty, even in uncertainty. You have mastered not only your external world, but more importantly, your inner world. Through the Life Mastery journey, you have stepped into your true power. You've found your purpose—not as a destination, but as a way of being.

Your heart and mind are no longer at odds. You've learned to listen inwardly, to follow your Soul's desires, and to stand firmly in your knowing. You've cultivated a calm that doesn't vanish in chaos.

You've learned how to return to joy at will, to find the center in every storm. You've discovered that peace isn't something you chase; it's something you *choose*, again and again. And you've made that choice your new way of life.

Regardless of what life places before you—loss or triumph, silence or applause—you've built the capacity to remain grounded, grateful, and open-hearted. That is your superpower: the ability to feel it all, and still return home to peace and happiness.

You are no longer the person who doubted your worth, second-guessed your intuition, or silenced your voice to make others comfortable. You are now the embodiment of purpose in motion—a being aligned, alive, and deeply anchored in truth. You walk in grace. Your mind is your ally. Your emotions are your compass. And your spirit? Unshakable.

Using the Life Mastery System, you've unlocked a portal into your highest self. You learned to manage your inner world so powerfully that the outer world began to respond in kind. Time, once slipping through your fingers, now expands to support your creativity and peace. You've streamlined your work and life with such clarity that abundance flows to you with grace and ease—income, yes, but also energy, opportunities, and soul-aligned partnerships.

You've let go of the old storylines—those dusty, hand-me-down beliefs that said you had to work hard for your money, sacrifice, or shrink to be worthy. You've released the need to be needed and any fear of failure. You no longer carry the weight of "not enough." You traded it for inner wisdom, strength, and excellence.

Now? Your life is a reflection of inner mastery. Mornings begin with stillness and intention. Your work flows from a deep well of purpose, not pressure. You create with joy, speak with conviction, and rest without guilt. You're healthier than you ever imagined possible—because you've chosen nourishment on every level. Your home is your sanctuary, your relationships are rich with authenticity, and your days are spacious, sacred, and joyfully designed.

You live in harmony with the laws of the Universe. You are magnetic. You are radiant. You are free.

And the most beautiful part? You're just getting started.

There are no limits here, only deeper truths to uncover, greater joy to embrace, and more lives to touch.

So wherever you are right now—whether you're truly just beginning or already in motion—know this: You are not becoming someone else. You are returning to the person you were always meant to be.

Keep listening to that still small voice within. Keep choosing joy. Keep walking the path and trusting the process. You've already come a long way, Keep going.

With awe and admiration,

I am that which you are becoming...

ABOUT THE AUTHOR

Wanda Marie is a writer, and author of several self-help books. She's a Certified Master Coach through the Behavioral Coaching Institute, and a life-long student and teacher of the metaphysical principles and universal laws that govern our lives. She is the founder of The LadyUp Network, an online platform dedicated to empowering women through affordable training programs, resources, and community.

Wanda Marie is an intuitive who blends the practical with the mystical. Her deep connection to the spiritual essence of life, cultivated since early childhood, led her to study various Western religions and Eastern philosophies, thereby cultivating her own spiritual foundation. She spent more than 12 years as a Licensed Spiritual Counselor through the Agape International Spiritual Center, and has traveled to the ancient land of Greece, **celebrated Amma's (**Mata Amritanandamayi**)** 50th birthday in Southern India, and meditated with spiritual leaders inside the Great Pyramids in Egypt.

Wanda Marie has dedicated her life to empowering women to better themselves and lead amazing lives. Learn more about her work by visiting www.ladyupnetwork.com.

Notes to ponder ~ thoughts to share

Life Mastery

Notes to ponder ~ thoughts to share

Notes to ponder ~ thoughts to share

Notes to ponder ~ thoughts to share

Notes to ponder ~ thoughts to share

Life Mastery

Notes to ponder ~ thoughts to share

Notes to ponder ~ thoughts to share

Life Mastery

Notes to ponder ~ thoughts to share

Notes to ponder ~ thoughts to share

www.ingramcontent.com/pod-product-compliance
Lightning Source LLC
Chambersburg PA
CBHW051128160426
43195CB00014B/2390